MARIO LEMIEUX
2001

Sports Illustrated

THE PENGUINS AT 50

PARTS OF THIS EDITION WERE PUBLISHED
PREVIOUSLY BY SPORTS ILLUSTRATED

FRONT COVER
Sidney Crosby
*Photograph by Al
Tielemans; Mario
Lemieux Photograph by
Bruce Bennett Studios/
Getty Images;* Jaromir
Jagr *Photograph by
Steve Babineau/NHLI/
Getty Images;* Evgeni
Malkin *Photograph by
Phillip MacCallum/
Getty Images*

BACK COVER
Marc-Andre Fleury
in 2016 *Photograph by
Graig Abel/NHLI/
Getty Images*

TITLE PAGE
Mario Lemieux
*Photograph by Keith
Srakocic/AP*

THIS PAGE
Sidney Crosby in 2016
*Photograph by Al Bello/
Getty Images*

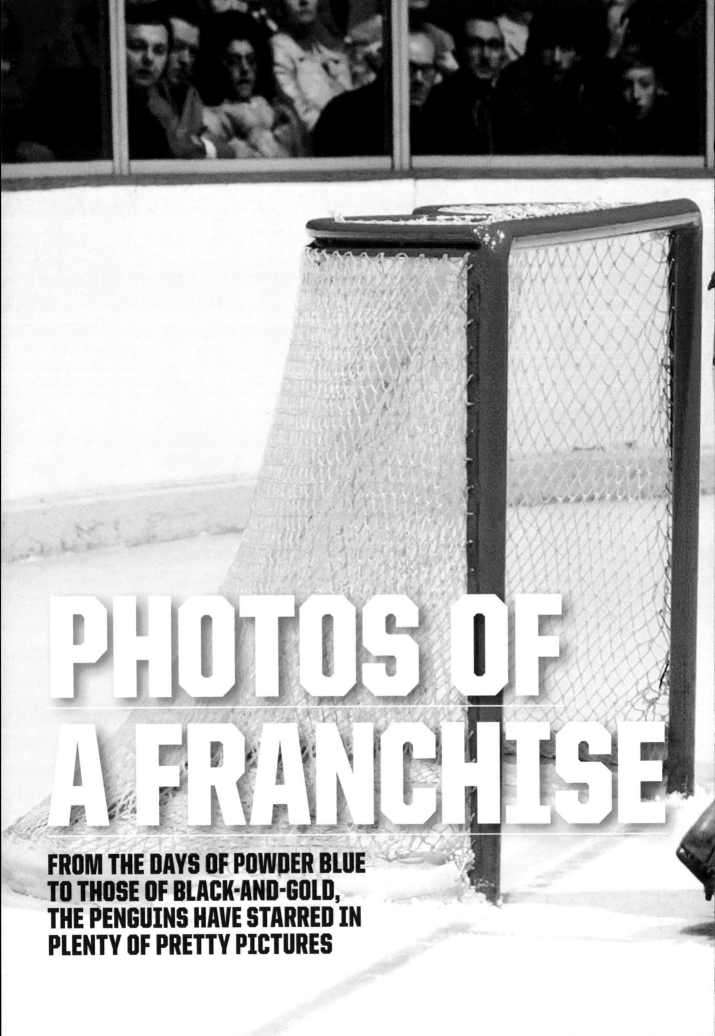

PHOTOS OF A FRANCHISE

FROM THE DAYS OF POWDER BLUE TO THOSE OF BLACK-AND-GOLD, THE PENGUINS HAVE STARRED IN PLENTY OF PRETTY PICTURES

ZOO CREW
Mario Lemieux made friends with his feathered counterparts in this photo shoot during his Calder-winning rookie season.

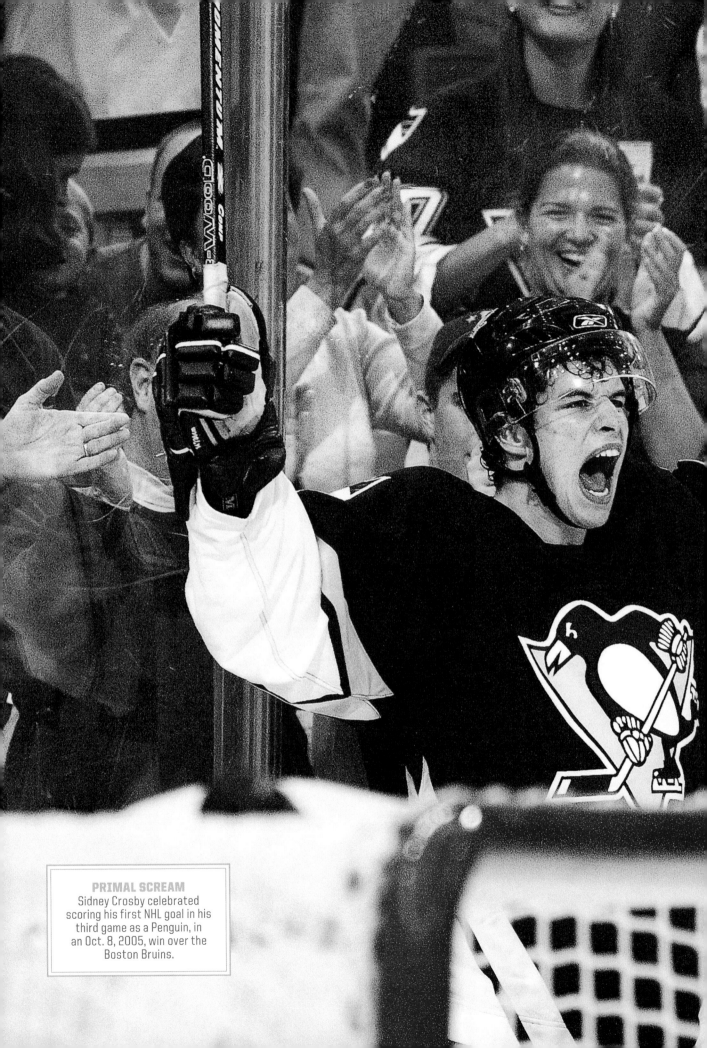

PRIMAL SCREAM
Sidney Crosby celebrated scoring his first NHL goal in his third game as a Penguin, in an Oct. 8, 2005, win over the Boston Bruins.

WING FLIP
Evgeni Malkin sent Detroit's
Darren Helm flying in Game 7
of the 2009 finals; Malkin was
named playoff MVP and the
Penguins won their third Cup.

COLOR GUARD
Goalie Gary Inness
took on the Islanders in
1974-75, the strongest
of the teams from the
Penguins' blue period.

INTRODUCTION

THE SECOND SIX

Fifty years ago the NHL doubled its size by adding six teams, with the Penguins growing into the strongest of the group

BY MICHAEL FARBER

O N FEB. 9, 1966, your favorite Mom-and-Pop puck shop demolished the walls and announced its coming-soon grand reopening as the big box store of hockey. With a historic vote the National Hockey League went continent-wide, doubling in size and ambition, capturing the American zeitgeist and fans in six new if sometimes fragile markets.

You remember when Dorothy lands in Oz and black-and-white bursts into glorious Technicolor?

The Second Six was the NHL's *Wizard of Oz* moment.

Looking back now, more than 50 years from that fateful day, president Clarence Campbell and the owners might seem like visionaries. That probably is giving this gang too much credit. They acted out of circumstance, not out of any cohesive vision. The $2 million expansion fee—almost $15 million in 2016 dollars, or some $485 million less than the Vegas Golden Knights are paying to be a proud partner of the NHL's Original 31 beginning next season—was catnip for fat cats in thrall of Major League Baseball's migration to California and in fear of a challenge from the old Western Hockey League. Prodded by New York Rangers president William M. Jennings, a longtime expansion proponent, Original Six owners finally caught the wave that had ushered in the sea change sweeping sports. In 1966, Joe Willie Namath of the American Football League's New York Jets was throwing the ball all over his shag-carpeted kingdom. The American Basketball Association, with its crazy red-white-and-blue ball and three-point shot, was in the pipeline. Major League Baseball was up to 20 teams. The cozy National House League had no choice but to grow. The decision gave

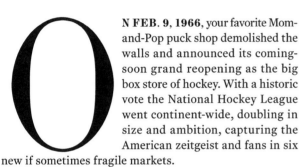

With a historic vote the NHL went continent-wide, capturing the American zeitgeist and fans in six new if sometimes fragile markets.

life to the Penguins, who played their first game on Oct. 11, 1967, hosting the Montreal Canadiens.

You might say the Second Six broke the color barrier. Willie O'Ree had done that on the ice in 1958 with the Boston Bruins, but we're talking about literal color, America's expanding palette. Although 97% of American households had only black-and-white TVs in 1964, by the time the Second Six began play in October '67 the three major networks were all televising their prime-time schedules in what was known as living color. The '60s: a kaleidoscope of Peter Max murals, flowers in the hair and kitchen appliances that could be purchased in avocado. The Original Six favored basic blue (Toronto Maple Leafs and the Rangers), red (Detroit Red Wings and Chicago Blackhawks) or both (Montreal Canadiens). (The black-and-gold Bruins were outliers.) Now came a Second Six riot of color: orange in Philadelphia, various shades of green in the Twin Cities and Oakland, purple—excuse me, Forum blue—in Los Angeles and a shade of blue in Pittsburgh that previously had been the domain of religious statuary and baby blankets.

As the Original Six owners heard expansion applicants during three days of presentations, it became clear that adding two or four teams made less sense than doubling down. Certainly a California team would need a nearby rival. Hockey-proud Minnesota, a state that had produced such seminal American players as old Blackhawks defenseman John Mariucci, seemed a fertile market, one that would benefit from having another Midwest sparring partner. St. Louis was the choice, but its inclusion was as much a real estate play as a hockey one. The Blackhawks' Arthur Wirtz and the Red Wings' James Norris had owned the St. Louis Arena since 1947 and wanted to unload it; as a condition of getting a franchise, Blues ownership agreed to purchase the ramshackle barn for an additional $4 million. Of course St. Louis already had had an NHL franchise, in '34–35, the star-crossed Eagles. Philadelphia also previously had its own one-year NHL wonder, the Quakers, who went 4-36-4 in '30–31 and then slunk into oblivion. The Quakers started in '25 as the Pittsburgh Pirates but moved cross-state because they had outgrown antiquated Duquesne Garden. In '80, when the Penguins petitioned to ditch beatific blue for their modern colors, they won their case over the howls of Bruins president Harry Sinden because the hockey Pirates originally had worn black and gold.

So the Second Six was undeniably colorful, even if the mess in those first few years looked like a kindergartner's finger painting. Consider the Kings' actual arrival in Los Angeles in 1967. As the team staggered off a TWA flight at LAX, "Cowboy" Bill Flett emerged with a 10-gallon Stetson, Réal (Frenchy) Lemieux wore a beret and Bryan (Chief) Campbell sported a Native American headdress. (In the '60s, only stereotypes flourished as much as color.) At the first practice at Long Beach Arena, the equipment managers couldn't find any pucks. A Canadian, a Smothers Brothers Comedy Hour producer named Saul Ilson, who happened to be the stands, saved the day. He summoned a gofer to fetch a signed puck from his office that had been a gift from Canadiens' Hall of Fame winger Boom Boom Geoffrion. So less than an hour later, Los Angeles practiced. With one autographed puck. Until Marcel Dionne arrived in 1975, you could have made an argument that the Kings didn't much need a puck, anyway.

Of course the embryonic Kings were models of stability compared to the Bay Area gong show. The expansion team began life as the California Seals. A month after the home opener, it changed to the Oakland Seals. If coach and general manager Bert Olmstead had had his way, the team would have been called the Vancouver Seals; Olmstead kept lobbying for a move to Canada. (Pro tip: This is not how you make a good first impression.) They were on their third name, the California Golden Seals, by 1970. Charles O. Finley was the owner then. He wanted to ditch green-and-gold skates for white ones, like the white spikes worn by his Oakland A's. The idea quickly was consigned to the dustbin of hockey history, not unlike the Seals themselves. In 1976 the franchise migrated east to become the Cleveland Barons, who two years later merged with the scuffling Minnesota North Stars. Of the original Second Six, four remain.

There were trying decades for the Second Six—the Blues flirted with moving to Saskatoon, of all places, in 1983—but ultimately the Penguins, on the cusp of relocation at least three times themselves, emerged as the most resounding success. The Flyers won a Stanley Cup first, in 1974 and again in '75, but Pittsburgh's four championships are as many as the remaining Second Six franchises combined. (The Kings, like Philadelphia, have two.) The Penguins won back-to-back Cups, in 1991 and '92, but also won in each succeeding decade, beating Detroit in a seven-game series in 2009 and San Jose in '16.

Truly, Pittsburghers are spoiled. They have feasted on

HAPPY DAYS
The Penguins celebrated topping defending champ Detroit in 2009 for the third of the franchise's four Cups.

DAVID E. KLUTHO

hockey eye candy, three of the world's best forwards of the past half-century: Mario Lemieux, Sidney Crosby and Jaromir Jagr. They were all drafted high and yet all arrived by different paths. Scouting acumen snagged Jagr fifth overall in 1990. Crosby, the incandescent junior star, came via serendipity in 2005; the Penguins had three balls in the postlockout draft lottery. And Lemieux, godfather of the modern franchise,

was a by-product of skullduggery. In 1984 general manager Ed Johnston did all he could to ensure Pittsburgh finished last in that pre-lottery era, including trading former Norris Trophy defenseman Randy Carlyle and demoting goalie Roberto Romano because he had the temerity to win a few games. Tanks, for the memories.

Lemieux revived a moribund franchise in 1984 and again in 2000 when he came out of retirement to rejoin the team of which he had become part owner. (In his first game back, Lemieux had an assist 33 seconds into his opening shift.) Having twice been in Chapter 11, the now bedrock franchise writes happier chapters in the NHL's most dazzling rink, the recently renamed PPG Paints Arena.

There is your Second Six color.　　　　□

STAR POWER
Evgeni Malkin controlled the puck against Sean Couturier (14) and Jakub Voracek (93) in a regular-season game in Philadelphia in 2012.

V.

50 YEARS OF HATE

The Pennsylvania pair from the Second Six have shown a penchant for in-state infighting

FROM CLASHES between Mario Lemiuex and Eric Lindros in the 1990s to a five-overtime game in the 2000 playoffs to the teams' brawl-filled 2012 playoff series with 312 penalty minutes, the Flyers have become the Penguins' fiercest rival. Pittsburgh can boast greater team success, winning four Stanley Cups to Philadelphia's two (with none since '75), but the Flyers have been pesky in head-to-head match-ups. Thanks to a lead built up in the 1970s, the Flyers held a 151-89-30-8 regular-season lead heading into the Feb. 25 clash at Heinz Field.

FIRST CONTACT
Mario Lemieux challenged goalie Ron Hextall in the first playoff meeting between the teams, in 1989. While Pittsburgh has had more overall postseason success, Philadelphia has proved to be a tough out over the years.

GEORGE TIEDEMANN/GT IMAGES

MUG SHOT
Peter Popovic took down the Flyers' John LeClair during a Penguins win in Game 1 of the 2000 conference semifinals, a series that would include a five-overtime marathon.

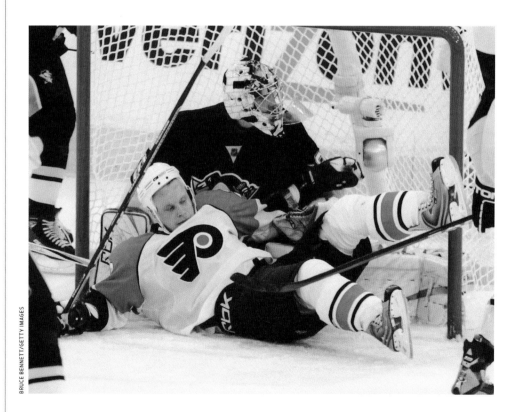

DUMPED
Marc-Andre Fleury tangled with Philly's Lasse Kukkonen in Game 2 of the 2008 conference finals. The Penguins won the game and the series.

LEN REDKOLES/NHL/GETTY IMAGES

BRAWL TIME
The fight-filled Game 3 of the 2012 conference quarterfinals featured 158 penalty minutes; among those who mixed it up were Craig Adams and the Flyers' Scott Hartnell (top and bottom) and Kris Letang and Kimmo Timonen (middle).

BRUCE BENNETT/GETTY IMAGES

TOM MIHALEK/AP

STAR STRUCK
In a playoff fight with unusually high star power, Sidney Crosby took down the Flyers' Claude Giroux in Game 3.

BRUCE BENNETT/GETTY IMAGES

BECOMING CHAMPIONS

**THE PENGUINS SURVIVED
SHAKY YEARS TO FIND SUCCESS
TIME AND TIME AGAIN**

FLIGHT RISK

They were winners (at last!), they were entertaining—but were they headed out of town?

BY MARK MULVOY

From Sports Illustrated
April 28, 1975

T**OO BAD**, Pittsburgh. Just when the Penguins produce a winning hockey team, just when a 19-year-old named Pierre Larouche is as big an autograph in the Golden Triangle as the Steelers' Franco Harris or the Pirates' Willie Stargell, just when scholarly goaltender Gary Inness pulls a Mazeroski on another team from New York, just when Dave Burrows perfects his Mean Joe Greene act on defense, they all may be departing for Denver or Seattle—and not just for a short holiday.

On the ice the Pittsburgh franchise has become as solid as the vaults at Mellon Bank. The Penguins, who in seven previous seasons never had come close to winning as many games as they lost, started this season as a no-name gang plus Vic Hadfield. Eighty games later they were at 37-28-15, the sixth-best record in the 18-team NHL. And along the way some of the no-names lost their anonymity, e.g.: center Syl Apps, MVP in the All-Star Game; the irrepressible M. Larouche, the league's flashiest rookie; the fidgety Inness, who leads Ken Dryden three degrees to two in hockey's brain race; and the sturdy Burrows, the game's best defensive defenseman. In the first round of the Stanley Cup playoffs the Penguins briskly dispatched the hated St. Louis Blues in two straight games. Then, thanks to Inness's uncanny stand-up shot blocking, they streaked to three straight wins over the New York Islanders last week, but the Islanders staved off elimination Sunday afternoon with a 3–1 victory.

Off the ice the Penguins are an endangered species. The club is more than $3 million deep in red ink, not including its

DENIS BRODEUR/NHL/GETTY IMAGES

BLUE STAR
Gary Inness's strength in goal was a key to the franchise's first winning season, as the Penguins went 37-28-15 in 1974-75.

delinquencies to the NHL, and will be moved to either Denver or Seattle at the end of the playoffs unless team president Tad Potter finds fresh investors. "I don't dare go out to lunch anymore," says Potter. "I've got to stay close to my phone in case a potential buyer calls. My close friend Peter Burchfield, my mother, my cousin and her husband, my aunt and I have 66% of the stock and, thus, control of the team. The rest of the ownership is well spread out. In fact, 25 guys own a total of 5%, and I know they're scattered all over the country. At the start I tried to solve the financial problems in such a way that I could retain control, but I'm afraid it's not possible. In today's climate no investor will pour $3 million into something without acquiring control. So I'm ready to bite the bullet."

Back in January the NHL leaked word that the Pittsburgh franchise would be transferred if there were not an immediate upsurge in both attendance at the Civic Arena and investor interest shown by local moneymen. When he returned from the Super Bowl, Pittsburgh mayor Peter Flaherty called a breakfast meeting of civic leaders and organized a "Save the Penguins" drive. His wife, Nancy, took an office alongside Potter's and spent weeks phoning the presidents of local companies, imploring them to purchase blocks of tickets for the remaining Penguins games. Nancy's sweet talk obviously worked, for Pittsburgh's average attendance jumped from 10,117 to 12,885 for the last 17 games. Better still, the Penguins have attracted capacity-plus crowds of more than 13,000 for each of their three home playoff games.

But local investors are still not reaching for their wallets. "I don't understand it," Potter says. "The club's going well, they're adding 3,000 seats to the building, and still nothing has happened here. The three groups I'm talking to now are from Philadelphia, Seattle and New York. Who knows what they'll do if they buy control?"

There are no hidden reasons for the financial plight of the Penguins. The small capacity of the Civic Arena ensures nickel-and-dime-sized profits even with full houses, and in 1972, when the NHL-WHA war inflated player salaries more than 100%, the Penguins began to report annual losses of up to $1 million. The club's cash-flow position is so bad that it recently held a flea-market sale of used equipment, pulling more than $2,500. At the same time the Penguins were an inferior product on the ice until crafty Jack Button took over as general manager midway through the 1973–74 season and brought in fiery Marc Boileau as coach.

"We were hardly an entertaining team," Button says. "We had Burrows on defense and the line of Apps, [Jean] Pronovost and [Lowell] MacDonald. That was all." Living on the phone, Button acquired tough guys Bob (Battleship) Kelly, Steve Durbano and Bob Paradise, and for the first time the Penguins started to hit back. Inness was moved up from Canadian college ranks after a short stop in Hershey; then Button obtained Vic Hadfield and his $200,000 per year contract from the New York Rangers.

FLASH POINTS
Larouche scored 68 points as a rookie in 1974-75; the next year, at age 20, he surpassed 100 points, then the youngest player ever to do so.

"What we still didn't have," Button says, "was a player who would get the fans out of their seats. We had a lot of good steady hockey players, the guys you need to win. We didn't have anyone with flair." Enter Pierre Larouche of Amos, Quebec.

Larouche has flair. He was 18 years old at the time of the draft and the Montreal Canadiens called to say that they were thinking about making him one of their five first-round picks. "Don't bother," Larouche said. "If you draft me, you'll send me right to the minor leagues. I'm good enough to play in the NHL now. If you draft me, I'll sign with the World Hockey Association." Forewarned, the Canadiens passed on Larouche, and Button made him Pittsburgh's No. 1 selection and the eighth pick in the entire draft. Two days later Button received a telegram: YOU ARE INVITED TO ATTEND THE FIRST ANNUAL PIERRE LAROUCHE INVITATIONAL GOLF TOURNAMENT IN AMOS, QUEBEC. BRING YOUR OWN CLUBS. PIERRE.

Larouche, who carries a one handicap, introduced himself to the Penguins by beating Hadfield, a golf pro in the off-season, in the club's training-camp tournament. "Vic said I cheated, that I moved the ball with my foot in the rough," Larouche says. "So we played again, and I beat him again. He had another excuse that time, but I forget what it was."

In Pittsburgh the baby-faced Larouche naturally has been the target of many of his teammates' jokes. One day Battleship Kelly invited Larouche to join him for a postpractice drink at the Jamestown Inn. When the waiter brought them their beers, Kelly warned him not to serve Larouche because he was under age. Another day Paradise complained that Boileau had scheduled a 2 p.m. practice because "Pierre doesn't get out of school until 1:30." However, when the needling gets too personal, Larouche will silence a mate like Hadfield by reminding him, "When I was a little kid, Vic, I used to watch you on television."

Larouche quickly captivated the crowds in Pittsburgh with his smooth skating, precise stickhandling and quick, hard shots. There is some Jean Beliveau in his erect skating stride, some Stan Mikita in his deft moves with a stick and some Phil Esposito in his quick reactions around the net. Playing regularly between Kelly and Chuck Arnason, Larouche scored 31 goals and had 37 assists for 68 points to lead the NHL rookies. "Like most young kids," he says, "I'm a little cocky. Hey, I believe in myself. Am I the best rookie? Sure I am. Why should I say that someone else is the best rookie?"

Near the end of the season a radio station sponsored a "Date with Pierre" contest in which the winner would indeed get a date with Larouche. There were more than 1,500 entrants, including grandmothers, mothers, daughters and a four-year-old girl. Larouche met the winner, 20-year-old Karen Ahearn, a secretary, at center ice. "And what is it," the announcer asked, "that a young Frenchman would say to a girl on their very first date?" Larouche laughed. "Voulez-vous coucher avec moi ce soir?" he said unabashedly. Maybe Pittsburgh's not ready for little Pierre. □

In June 1975, fresh off a postseason trip to the quarterfinals, the Penguins declared bankruptcy. But a month later the team was purchased by Al Savill, Otto Frenzel and Wren Blair, holding off the threat of relocation . . . for the moment.

A SAVIOR ARRIVES

Even when Mario Lemieux was just 20 years old, Pittsburgh already saw him as a transformative figure for the franchise

BY BOB KRAVITZ

FROM SPORTS ILLUSTRATED
MARCH 3, 1986

MMMMMM . . . egg rolls. Better yet, microwaved egg rolls. Mario Lemieux, the extraordinary young center for the Pittsburgh Penguins and our culinary guide for the evening, carefully fingers each icy morsel and then fires it into the oven.

"Something to drink?" he asks, opening the refrigerator. Inside, there is food with a Civil War expiration date. The dishes in the sink are dirty. On the bottom shelf of the fridge is a very dubious-looking chocolate cream pie. "My girlfriend made that," Lemieux says. "She went back home to Montreal three weeks ago."

Thank goodness beer keeps. Lemieux grabs an Iron City—what else would a self-respecting Pittsburgher drink—and plops down onto the couch in his furnished apartment. Soon the microwave whines. Lemieux, with the daring of youth, takes the first bite. "Ugggh," he says, wincing. "Bad, eh?" Lemieux does the only rational thing. Back to the refrigerator. Ketchup.

So now the ugly truth can be told. Lemieux is a normal 20-year-old, much like any other 20-year-old. Except for one difference: He's the 20-year-old who saved hockey in Pittsburgh, the man-child who brought the Penguins back from endangered species status, both competitively and financially. No player—not Wayne Gretzky, not Bobby Orr—has ever been asked to do so much both on the ice and off. No player has ever responded more brilliantly and gracefully.

"Without Lemieux, they pack up the team and move to another city," says Glen Sather, president, general manager and coach of the Edmonton Oilers.

Lemieux, drafted No. 1 overall in 1984, won the Calder Trophy as the NHL's Rookie of the Year. He was the Most Valuable Player in the All-Star Game. And, moonlighting, he led Team Canada to a stunning victory over the Soviet Union and a second-place finish at the world championships in Prague.

This season Lemieux is ahead of that pace, and perhaps most important, the Penguins are no longer regarded by Pittsburgh as comic relief after the Steelers pack up and go home. Last season, attendance at the 16,033-seat Civic Arena increased 46%, from an average of 6,839 to 10,018. This season there has been another 18% gain, to 11,864. How much of that increase is due to Lemieux? "I'd say 90%," says Paul Steigerwald, the Penguins' director of marketing. "No, actually I'd have to say 100%. Without him, the team doesn't improve and the fans don't come out. He's meant everything to this organization."

Including its continued existence in Pittsburgh. It was only last summer that Edward J. DeBartolo, owner of the Penguins and the Major Indoor Soccer League's Pittsburgh Spirit, threatened to disband or move both of the financially draining franchises. The Penguins were said to be going north across the border to Hamilton, Ont. But on July 22, DeBartolo won a $425,000 reduction in Civic Arena rent and a city-county commitment of as much as $11.4 million to refurbish the 24-year-old building. In return, DeBartolo pledged only to keep the teams in Pittsburgh for at least this season. Now, with Lemieux leading a renaissance, the moving vans have been called off. "We're staying right here," says general manager Eddie Johnston.

ON LOCATION
The latest rumors had the Penguins moving to Canada before Lemieux came along to save Pittsburgh hockey.

And so is Lemieux. He had signed the richest NHL rookie contract ever—$350,000 for each of his first two seasons. This winter the Penguins gave him a five-year deal worth an estimated $2.75 million, which puts him second only to Gretzky on the league salary scale.

A small price to pay for a savior. "Look at him," says Michel Goulet of the Quebec Nordiques pointing toward Lemieux, who towers over a clot of reporters. Members of both All-Star teams are gathered for a press conference at the University of Connecticut Health Center in Hartford on the day before their recent game. "Nothing bothers him," says Goulet, who is, like Lemieux, a French Canadian acquainted with the problems of expressing himself accurately in English. "He's so calm."

Lemieux draws questions he has heard many times before: How do you compare with Gretzky? . . . Do you feel any different this year than last year? . . . Are you excited about the All-Star Game?

Lemieux responds patiently: I'm not at the same level as Gretzky yet. . . . Yes, I feel more comfortable this year. . . . Sure, I'm excited. It's the best against the best. It'll be fun.

Lemieux takes the responsibilities of superstardom seriously. "It is something he's prepared for, because people have been talking about him since he was very young," says Gretzky, who was a household name in Canada when he was nine. "The hardest part is that sometimes people forget you're human."

There's the hitch. Lemieux is just 20. Adulthood doesn't just knock on the door and let itself in after you score your first NHL goal—which Lemieux did on his very first shift for the Penguins. "Mario sort of has a dual personality," says Bob Perno, one of Lemieux's agents. "Around the people he doesn't really know or people in the hockey world—teammates and reporters—he has an image he must project. And he knows that. Always smiling, taking things in stride. He has unbelievable maturity in that sense, a 20-year-old going on 28.

"But when you get him away from that scene, get him back home with friends, he reverts to being an 18-year-old. I remember the night before we signed his new contract this winter. There was still a lot of pressure. I was nervous, his dad was nervous. So we're sitting there in his apartment and Mario says, 'Let's play Intellivision Football.' I swear, he was more interested in beating me at Intellivision Football than he was about a multimillion-dollar contract. That's the flip side."

Ever since his first glimpse of downtown Pittsburgh from the mouth of the Fort Pitt Tunnel, Lemieux has been hooked on the town. He wants to make it his permanent home, to the Penguins' delight. "This is the guy we're building the franchise around," says Johnston.

Not a bad idea. After all, what other city has a young center who can be legitimately compared with the Great One? Gretzky versus Lemieux. Sather says it's unfair. Johnston calls it premature, though he will not let the subject drop until he has built a persuasive case for Lemieux as this year's league MVP.

MATTER OF SCALE
In 1986 players around the league were starting to fully grasp the difficulty of containing the 6' 4", 230-pound Lemieux.

Gretzky is finding the speculative matchups a bit tedious. "It seems like only yesterday people were saying I was too small and too slow to play this game," he says. "Now, all of a sudden I'm over the hill."

There is one basis for comparison in which Gretzky clearly comes off second best; at 6 feet and 170 pounds, he gives away four inches and 30 pounds to Lemieux. And Lemieux makes the most of the difference. Since the second half of last season Lemieux's game has become more physical. "Winning the All-Star Game MVP gave him the confidence that he belonged," says Johnston. "From then on, he took off." Says coach Bob Berry, "He might be the best defensive forward we have. He was never asked to play defensively in the juniors, but Mario realizes that he has to play both ends of the ice in this league and he has done it quite well. He comes back deep into his own end and he takes the body." Actually, it is more apt to compare Lemieux with the most classic center in hockey history, Jean Beliveau, the cornerstone of the Montreal dynasty from 1950 to '71. Lemieux could be the next great "big man" in hockey. "Mario's strength gives his game a whole different dimension," says Philadelphia coach Mike Keenan. "He can do more than just finesse you; he can beat you with his size. That's why he's so effective in tight situations around the net."

Lemieux's puck-handling dexterity and his long reach make him especially dangerous in cramped quarters. At times Lemieux appears to be playing shinny when he senses a teammate cutting toward the net. Then zap.

"If you go at Mario like a madman, he'll make you look like a complete idiot," says Bruins defenseman Ray Bourque. "He just holds the puck out there on his forehand and dares to you to commit yourself." Lemieux's game is a study in self-control. He does not appear to play furiously; his arms and legs do not flail madly. "He's a very deceptive skater," says Philadelphia's Ron Sutter, one of Lemieux's designated shadows this season. "Believe me, when he wants to go, he goes."

"Walter Gretzky gave it to Wayne," says Sather. "Jean-Guy Lemieux gave it to Mario." Sather was just talking about one quality, talent. But Jean-Guy also gave his son a name that means "the best." In every way, Mario is living up to his inheritance. □

ON TOP OF THE WORLD

The 1991 Stanley Cup cemented Pittsburgh's rise and made obvious the absurdity of the criticism that Mario Lemieux was not a winner

BY JAY GREENBERG

FROM SPORTS ILLUSTRATED
JUNE 3, 1991

A FRANCHISE THAT suffered through nearly a quarter century of incompetence, that once had its office doors padlocked by the Internal Revenue Service and that in 1984 placed its last hope for survival in the hands of an 18-year-old named Mario Lemieux just saw its entire sorry history smoothed over with Zamboni-like precision. Led by Lemieux, the Pittsburgh Penguins won the Stanley Cup by routing the Minnesota North Stars 8–0 in Game 6 of the final series. Afterward, Lemieux was awarded the Conn Smythe Trophy as the MVP of the playoffs. Then, as proud as any captain who ever held the Cup aloft—and, at 6' 4", taller than most of them—he hoisted it as high as it has ever been hoisted.

Certainly few players have ever been required to lift a franchise the way Lemieux was asked to lift the Penguins, who until this season had not advanced beyond the second round in postseason play. "There wasn't going to be hockey in Pittsburgh anymore if not for Mario," said goalie Tom Barrasso. "And we wouldn't have won the Cup without him."

Lemieux had five goals and seven assists in the championship series, despite sitting out Game 3 with back spasms. He wound up with at least one point in each of his last 18 playoff games, and he scored at least one goal in each of his last 10. In Game 2 of the series against Minnesota, he had a breathtaking one-on-one goal that reversed the momentum of the game, which

the Penguins went on to win 4–1 to tie the series. In Game 5, he scored a goal and set up two more in a four-goal first-period blitz that gave Pittsburgh a 6–4 victory and control of the series. Finally, with the Penguins leading 1–0 in Game 6, Lemieux deflected a pass during a 5-on-3 Minnesota power play, then forced the Stars' Mike Modano to take him down. The resulting penalty eased the crisis to a mere 5-on-4. Moments later, Lemieux broke away and made three separate backhand-to-forehand moves en route to scoring a shorthanded goal that made it 2–0. He would add three assists.

At practically every pivotal moment against Minnesota, as well as in the Penguins' six-game triumph over the Boston Bruins in the Wales Conference finals, Lemieux responded with either a point or a strong shift. In the finals, he also played strong defense, continually bumped North Stars off the puck in the Pittsburgh zone and patrolled center ice like a minesweeper. "It seemed like anything that was within 20 feet he reached," said Minnesota's Dave Gagner. "When somebody that big and that good wants to win that badly, there isn't much you can do."

"We were hoping that Mario would be just regular," said North Star coach Bob Gainey, "but he wasn't." Instead, Lemieux was driven and dominant, exactly what his critics had insisted he would never be.

Lemieux has been trying to live up to extraordinary expectations since the Penguins made him the No. 1 selection in the 1984 draft. Lemieux, who is among the few players who possess a fifth gear, was generally content to play in fourth gear his first few seasons. Sure, he got his points—he scored 141 in '85–86—but Pittsburgh was slow to assemble talent around him and didn't make the playoffs his first four seasons.

Continued on page 41

LOOK WHO'S HERE
After missing Game 3 because of back spasms, Lemieux returned to help the Penguins take the last three games.

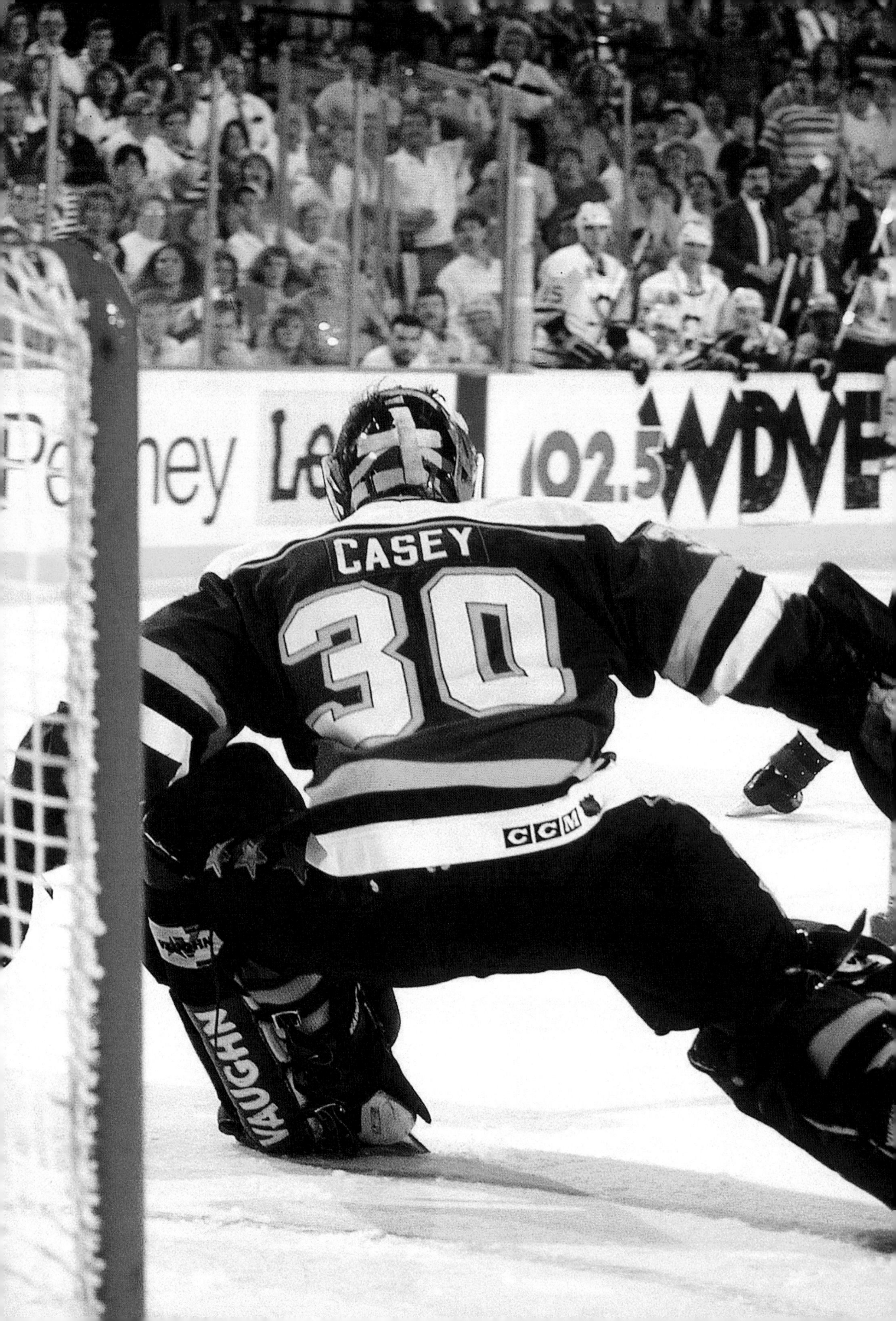

CASEY
30
102.5
WDVE
CCM
VAUGHN

COMING THROUGH
Lemieux, here scoring on the North Stars in Game 2 of the Cup finals, had at least one goal in each of his final 10 playoff games in '91.

Continued from page 37

Denied the experience of playing in big games, Lemieux had no understanding of the level he would have to reach to win them.

That changed in the 1987 Canada Cup, when Lemieux, challenged by world-class opposition and pushed by Team Canada linemate Wayne Gretzky, played with as much heart as talent, scored a tournament-high 11 goals and led Canada to victory. "He was a different person when he came back from that," says Pittsburgh forward Phil Bourque. Lemieux outscored Gretzky in each of the next two seasons and performed well in his first playoff appearance, as the Penguins reached the seventh game of the divisional finals in 1989.

Yet Lemieux's emergence as the game's premier talent while Gretzky was still near his peak offended large portions of the hockey world. It seemed impossible that such a gifted player could come along and challenge Gretzky's accomplishments so soon. Denial was a common reaction: There was no room for another player of Gretzky's caliber until the Great One's career had started to wind down.

Moreover, Gretzky won four Stanley Cups while with the Edmonton Oilers and brought the moribund Los Angeles Kings to life. These team achievements cemented his place as the greatest player of all time. Lemieux, on the other hand, had to deal with the trumped-up charge that he wasn't a winner. The evidence may have been circumstantial, but Lemieux had no way of disproving it with the woeful Penguins. "I don't care what people write and say about me," said Lemieux last Saturday night, "as long as I have the respect of my teammates."

The criticism "has to have hurt him a little," said defenseman Paul Coffey, one of Lemieux's closest friends on the Penguins, "but I know it would hurt him more if he had thought his teammates believed any of that stuff. He was going to hear it until he won a Stanley Cup. It was unfair, but that's just the way it goes."

It went that way even in Game 1 of the finals, in which Lemieux scored a short-handed goal but nonetheless faced raised eyebrows after the North Stars recovered to win 5–4. Not enough? Then how about that marvelous goal in Game 2 at Pittsburgh's Civic Arena.

The North Stars had scored early in the second period to cut a 2–0 Penguin lead in half when Lemieux commenced his improbable journey up-ice. Taking an outlet pass from Bourque, Lemieux roared in on defenseman Shawn Chambers, faked outside, cut inside, used his backhand to put the puck between Chambers's legs and then raced ahead to pick it up on his forehand. Minnesota goalie Jon Casey wisely waited for Lemieux to make the first move, but that didn't help. Lemieux took the puck to his forehand, switched it to his backhand and, while sliding to his knees, put the puck into an empty net. The sleight-of-hand required to complete the play at the speed Lemieux was traveling was astounding. The spectacle was also deflating for the North Stars, who had all but shut down Hull and other potent scorers in the first three rounds.

Two nights later at the Met

UP, IN ARMS
Veteran defenseman Gordie Roberts hoisted the Cup after the Game 6 win at the Met Center.

DAVID E. KLUTHO

Center, the same Lemieux who had left North Stars tumbling all over the ice as if their skate laces had been tied together, couldn't unfasten his own. Lemieux, who reported to the rink with stiffness in his back, tested it during warmups and decided he couldn't play. The spasms—which the Penguins insist are not related to the back surgery Lemieux underwent in July 1990 or to the subsequent infection that forced him to miss the first 50 games of this season—usually subside within a few hours if Lemieux doesn't try to play through them. Hoping to get Lemieux back for Game 4, the Penguins didn't push him to take the ice, and the result was predictable: Minnesota won 3–1 to take a 2–1 series lead.

The next day, Penguins coach Bob Johnson and general manager Craig Patrick refused to bring Lemieux—or any other player, for that matter—to a scheduled media session at the Met Center. However, a Pittsburgh reporter who had had difficulty catching up with Lemieux as Lemieux walked briskly uphill on a sidewalk near the Penguins' St. Paul hotel reported that a Game 4 comeback by Le Magnifique was looking strong. Most doubts about his ability to continue in the series were removed when he whisked in a goalmouth setup by Mark Recchi to climax a three-goal burst that gave Pittsburgh a 3–0 lead after only 2:58 of the first period. With Lemieux dishing out more than his share of bumps and getting to many of the loose pucks, Pittsburgh, which would prevail 5–3, survived a Minnesota rally and a five-minute penalty late in the third period before Bourque put the game away with an empty-net goal.

It was apparent in the first two shifts of Game 5 in Pittsburgh that Lemieux understood that the series was now his to win. In the first period, he went on a feeding frenzy. After Penguin defenseman Larry Murphy shot the puck wide of Casey, Lemieux grabbed the carom off the boards and went backhand-to-forehand to sweep the puck across the goal line before Casey could get to the post. With the score 2–0, Lemieux skated past Chambers and Gagner to create a 2-on-1 at the Minnesota blue line and then led Recchi perfectly with a backhand pass. Recchi converted with a bull's-eye over Casey's left shoulder. Later, Recchi made the score 4–0 by hitting the top of the net again, this time off a rebound created by Lemieux jamming at the cage. But as in the previous game, Pittsburgh squandered most of its lead and needed a late goal, this time from Troy Loney, to escape with a victory.

Though the North Stars performed pluckily enough to make all but Games 2 and 6 an adventure, the series wasn't always well played. Both teams took unnecessary penalties at key moments. Minnesota suffered several flat—and dooming—first periods, and the Penguins, while improved defensively, played fast and loose at times. Though Pittsburgh was as tight as it had to be when protecting a lead late in games and almost perfect throughout Game 6, its Cup triumph was hardly forged in the traditional manner—with defense. The Penguins won because they generated brilliant offensive bursts that the North Stars could not.

A lot of Penguins helped create the occasion, but it was Lemieux who rose to it. The long arms of the best player—in the series and on the planet—carried the Stanley Cup to Pittsburgh. □

DAVID E. KLUTHO (2)

1992 STANLEY CUP
Penguins beat Blackhawks
four games to none

WINNING DEFENSE
Tom Barrasso made
a save against Chicago
in a 3-1 win in
Game 2 of the 1992
Stanley Cup finals.

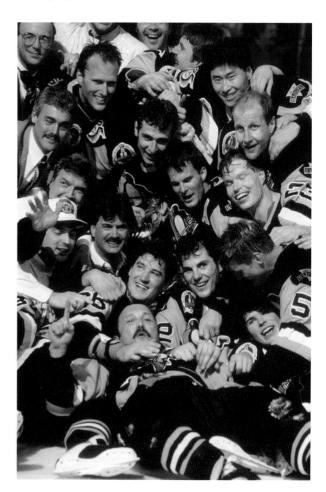

SWEEPS WEEK
The Penguins ran over
the Blackhawks in four
games, with Lemieux
winning his second
Conn Smythe award.

AS HOT AS IT GETS

The 1992–93 Penguins won
17 consecutive games,
an NHL record that still stands

BY JON SCHER

FROM SPORTS ILLUSTRATED
APRIL 19, 1993

THE GREATEST show on earth played Madison Square Garden twice last Friday, and only once was it the circus. The afternoon may have belonged to the jugglers and the clowns, but the night belonged to Mario Lemieux and the Pittsburgh Penguins.

By the time Lemieux had scored his fifth goal of the game—tying a career high—in a 10–4 rout of the New York Rangers, the Garden air was full of history and the rafters were ringing with cheers. Even the most partisan Rangers fans had to take the bags off their heads and appreciate what Lemieux and the Penguins had done, not only that night but over the last month as well.

The blowout of the Rangers gave Pittsburgh its 16th straight victory, breaking the NHL record for consecutive wins established by the 1981–82 New York Islanders. The Penguins extended the streak to 17 with a 4–2 defeat of the Rangers the following night in Pittsburgh. "We'd like to keep it going," said Penguin center Ron Francis after last Saturday's game, "and put the record out of reach."

For the 27-year-old Lemieux, the streak has represented a triumph of body and will. By all rights his season should have been finished in early January when doctors discovered that a lump on his neck was the first stage of Hodgkin's disease. He missed 23 games while undergoing radiation treatments, which left him looking like the victim of a bad sunburn and feeling as if he had been run over by a truck. Lemieux returned to the lineup on March 2, a month ahead of schedule.

DAVID E. KLUTHO

During the 17 wins, the first of which occurred on March 9, Lemieux scored 27 goals and assisted on 24 others. That gave him 157 points through last weekend, which means that with only one game remaining in the regular season, he has all but wrapped up his fourth scoring title.

While Lemieux was sidelined, Buffalo Sabres center Pat LaFontaine had come from 33 points behind to take a 12-point lead in the league scoring race. "I thought about it even during radiation," says Lemieux quietly. "I was determined to come back and regain the lead."

LaFontaine, who had 145 points at week's end, never really had a prayer. "I grew up watching Bobby Orr," says Pittsburgh power forward Kevin Stevens. "And Wayne Gretzky was phenomenal. But Mario is on another level."

Remarkably, the cancer has made Lemieux greater than the sum of his parts. After being viewed for years as a major figure in a minor sport, Lemieux now transcends hockey. He's being recognized as the world's dominant pro athlete.

And the Penguins may be the world's dominant pro team. With the start of the NHL playoffs this weekend they will begin their quest for their third straight Stanley Cup. Like the Islanders of Mike Bossy, Bryan Trottier, Denis Potvin and Billy Smith, who won four consecutive Cups between 1980 and '83, the Penguins of Lemieux, Stevens, Ulf Samuelsson and Tom Barrasso can intimidate opponents merely by showing up. "Certainly we're not satisfied with just winning the games," says Lemieux. "We've been playing some pretty good hockey, but we think we can play much better."

It's hard to imagine how. In their history-making game against the Rangers, Pittsburgh was as overwhelming as it ever was in either of its championship seasons. For example, during a five-minute New York power play in the second period, the only shot by either team came from Lemieux, who scored a shorthanded breakaway goal. That effectively killed both the penalty and the Rangers. "They're an explosive team," says New York goalie Mike Richter, who replaced Corey Hirsch to start the third period and was victimized for five goals. "They take advantage of any mistake."

Like Lemieux, the Penguins are seeing their legend grow. They won both their Stanley Cups after having struggled in the regular season, thereby earning a reputation for being a team that could throttle up at will. This season they've kept the hammer down. "We're in high gear," says forward Rick Tocchet. "We're ready for the playoffs. And we know that anything less than the Stanley Cup is going to be a failure."

Says defenseman Peter Taglianetti, who was reacquired from the expansion Tampa Bay Lightning last month, "We're out to prove that this is the best team the league has seen in a long, long time."

Lemieux says that he's still drained and sore from the radiation therapy, but the only outward sign of his mortality is a half-moon-shaped bald patch on the back of his head. And you only notice that when he takes off his helmet. In full gear he's Super Mario, number 66, the greatest show on earth. □

BIG THREE
The Penguins defeated Detroit in a seven-game series in 2009, as Fleury's saves (below) helped give Crosby a chance to raise the Cup.

LOU CAPOZZOLA

DAVID E. KLUTHO (2)

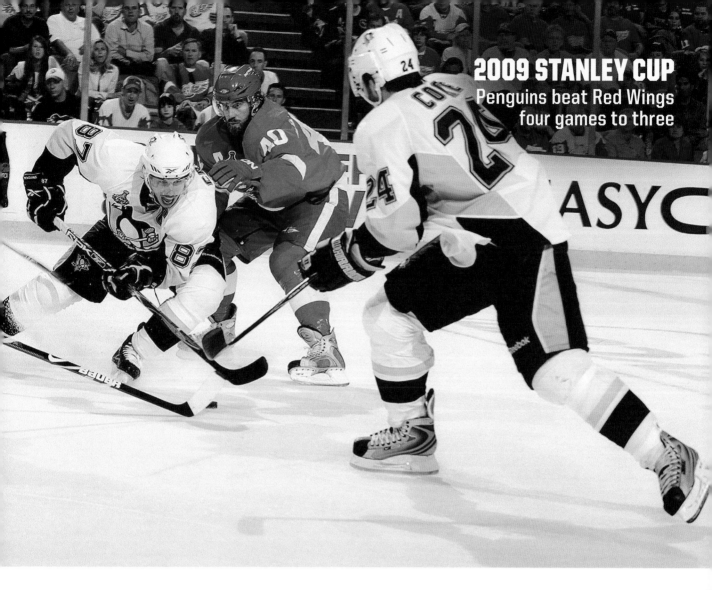

2009 STANLEY CUP
Penguins beat Red Wings
four games to three

2016 STANLEY CUP
Penguins beat Sharks four games to two

MVP ALERT
Sidney Crosby, the Conn Smythe winner for the 2016 postseason, faced off against San Jose's Logan Couture in Game 4 of the Stanley Cup finals (opposite).

TEAM WIN
Kris Letang (top) had a goal and four assists in the finals; Evgeni Malkin rejoiced with Ian Cole (28), Ben Lovejoy (12) and Matt Murray (30) (middle); Crosby again lifted the Cup.

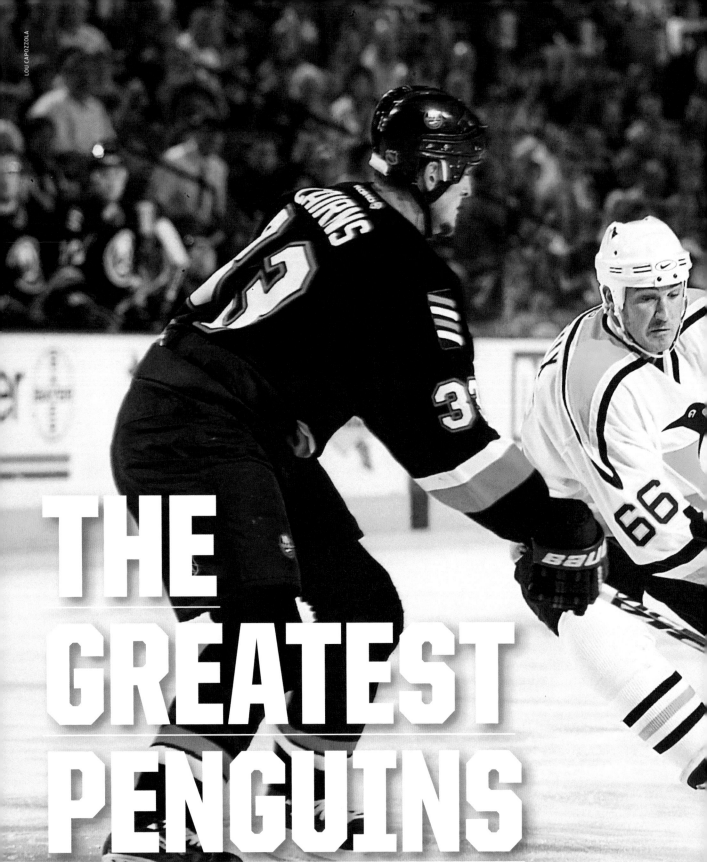

THE GREATEST PENGUINS

THE PLAYERS ON SI'S ALL-TIME TEAM AND IN THE GALLERY OF GREATS DEFINED HOCKEY IN PITTSBURGH

SI'S ALL-TIME PENGUINS TEAM

FIRST TEAM

MARIO LEMIEUX FORWARD
The franchise leader in just about every offensive category.

SIDNEY CROSBY FORWARD
His arrival in 2006 heralded the Penguins' return to the elite.

JAROMIR JAGR FORWARD
The gloriously mulleted Czech led the NHL in scoring five times as a Penguin.

PAUL COFFEY DEFENSEMAN
A great scorer from the blue line, he brought punch to the first Cup team.

ULF SAMUELSSON DEFENSEMAN
The 6' 1", 203-pound Robocop was as tough and nasty as they came.

TOM BARRASSO GOALIE
He delivered clutch performances in the 1991 and '92 postseasons.

SECOND TEAM

EVGENI MALKIN FORWARD
It's a sign of depth when a league MVP ends up on the second team.

RON FRANCIS FORWARD
The epitome of class led the NHL in assists twice and plus-minus in 1995.

KEVIN STEVENS FORWARD
He was an All-Star for those Cup winners in '91 and '92.

KRIS LETANG DEFENSEMAN
He's had three seasons scoring more than 50 points.

LARRY MURPHY DEFENSEMAN
The smart and low-key player gave the NHL the Murphy Dump.

MARC-ANDRE FLEURY GOALIE
The two-time All-Star holds most Penguins marks for the position.

PENGUINS LEADERS

GAMES PLAYED
MARIO LEMIEUX 915

GOALS
MARIO LEMIEUX 690

ASSISTS
MARIO LEMIEUX 1,033

POINTS
MARIO LEMIEUX 1,723

POINTS PER GAME
MARIO LEMIEUX 1.88

PLUS-MINUS
JAROMIR JAGR +207

GAME-WINNING GOALS
JAROMIR JAGR 78

PENALTY MINUTES
KEVIN STEVENS 1,084

WINS
MARC-ANDRE FLEURY 370

GOALS-AGAINST AVERAGE
MARC-ANDRE FLEURY 2.58

SHUTOUTS
MARC-ANDRE FLEURY 43

GREATEST PENGUINS

JEAN PRONOVOST
RW, 1968-78
The most consistent all-around player in the rough early years, the right wing was the first Penguin to top 100 points, in 1975-76.

STEVE BABINEAU/NHLI/GETTY IMAGES

BRUCE BENNETT/GETTY IMAGES

MICHEL BRIERE

C, 1969-70

A tragic story. Briere had shown great promise as a rookie, with 44 points, but after a car crash on May 15, 1970, he was in a coma for 11 months and died on April 13, 1971, at age 21.

STEVE BABINEAU/NHLI/GETTY IMAGES

SYL APPS JR.

C, 1970-77

Apps, the son of a Hall of Fame hockey player, led the Penguins in scoring for three consecutive seasons, from 1971-72 to '73-74, with a career-best 99 points in '73-74.

RANDY CARLYLE

D, 1978-84

A captain from 1981 to '84, Carlye is the only Penguin to win the Norris Trophy, which he did in 1980-81, when he led NHL defensemen in scoring with 83 points.

STEVE BABINEAU/NHLI/GETTY IMAGES

RICK KEHOE

RW, 1974-85

Fifth on the Penguins' all-time scoring list with 636 points, the clean-playing Kehoe was a two-time All-Star and won the Lady Bing Memorial Trophy in 1980-81.

STEVE BABINEAU/NHLI/GETTY IMAGES

MARIO LEMIEUX

In 2001 he emerged from three and a half years of retirement to become the hottest player, and ticket, in hockey

BY MICHAEL FARBER

FROM SPORTS ILLUSTRATED
MARCH 12, 2001

FOR MARIO LEMIEUX this wasn't a hockey game but an insult, one long Don Rickles routine at his expense. His linen-and-fine-china Pittsburgh Penguins were trailing 1–0 in the third period to the fries-with-that expansion Minnesota Wild, a team that had subdued the Penguins three days before and touched off an exchange of barbs between Lemieux and Minnesota coach Jacques Lemaire about the aesthetics of NHL hockey. The Wild embodies the trapping style of play that helped drive Lemieux out of hockey in 1997. Now, with nearly 13 minutes remaining, Lemieux decided he'd had enough. He was going to take this game and shake some sense into it. He retrieved the puck deep in the Pittsburgh zone and started out four-on-four, his body language screaming, This shall not pass.

Lemieux didn't quite go coast-to-coast. He lugged the puck over the Penguins' blue line, and then the red line, brushing off a hook by Marian Gaborik as if Gaborik were a piece of lint on his suit. As he crossed the Wild's blue line, he curled to create extra space and rifled the puck from 30 feet. The shot, from inside the right face-off circle, handcuffed goaltender Manny Fernandez and went in. It was a goal scorer's goal—a shot that pluggers would have buried in Fernandez's glove or pads. Nine minutes later, when Lemieux fired the puck toward the net from the right half boards, it struck a skate in front and caromed past Fernandez for the game-winner. This might not have been a battle for hockey's soul, but it wasn't a bad tussle for two points: Mario 2, Minnesota 1. Who's the hockey puck now?

There's only one real story in the NHL these days. From a standing start on Dec. 27, when he came out of a 3½-year retirement with a goal and two assists, Lemieux has been weaving through the scoring list like a New York City taxi. With 24 goals and 23 assists after a recent two-goal, two-assist performance in a 7–5 win over the New York Rangers, Lemieux had more points than anyone on Minnesota, Montreal or San Jose and more goals than the leaders of six NHL teams. Pittsburgh had averaged 1.14 more goals per game since he put the uniform back on—he'd figured in 41.6% of the Penguins' scores in that span—but even opponents had benefited from the return of Mario the Munificent. He'd played in 12 road games, and not a ticket to those matches had gone unsold, not even to games played in the usual sea of indifference in New Jersey or in the NHL's Shawshank, also known as the Nassau Coliseum, home of the inept New York Islanders. He might as well have parted the Red Sea.

"This is the best time of my life," Lemieux said recently, lingering in Pittsburgh's deserted dressing room after practice. "I had a lot of great moments in the early 1990s, but to be back and have a chance to play one more time has been great, especially with me playing well and the team playing well."

When Lemieux returned two months ago, his game was static and cerebral, a triumph of velvet hands and a Mensa head. He was playing left wing then, venturing no farther in his end than his blue line, loitering until a defenseman could find him with a breakout pass, preparing to saucer the puck to linemate Jaromir Jagr and maybe work a give-and-go. He was poetry in slow motion, running the game at his own meter. However, in the last several weeks Lemieux settled back in at center, and he has begun winning face-offs, deigning to backcheck, skating more, stretching his game on occasions to nearly 200 feet.

Lemieux, whose chronic back ailment was a factor in his retirement, felt his back seize up at practice on Feb. 9, touching off an understandable panic in Pittsburgh. But while the coccyx crowed and massage therapist Tommy Plasko worked overtime, something wonderful was happening elsewhere on Lemieux's body. His legs, heavy after the All-Star break, suddenly felt as fresh as they had in almost a decade. He was struck by an urge to grab the puck and go, to beat de-

C, 1984-97, 2000-06
The three-time league MVP is second in NHL history in career points per game, and his 1999 purchase of the team was instrumental in keeping the Penguins in Pittsburgh.

fenders one-on-one, to do substantially more than fill in the blanks. His legs carried him to that game-turner against Minnesota—"An old Mario goal, a late '80s-early '90s goal," Penguins defenseman Marc Bergevin called it—and to a rebound in overtime against the Devils two nights later that forced goalie Martin Brodeur, who had just foiled Jagr on a breakaway, to make a second save in a string as spectacular as any in his career.

Although skating hasn't been a cornerstone of Lemieux's game , his underrated speed can open up more offensive possibilities than he'd been opening since his return. Lemieux's

success has been almost freakish. The scary part is that until recently it has unfolded in second gear.

"My goal is to be better than I was in 1997," says Lemieux, who led the NHL in scoring in '96–97 with 122 points in 76 games. "I probably won't be as good as I was [in Pittsburgh's Stanley Cup years of '91 and '92, when he averaged 1.95 points per game], but I can get pretty close."

Lemieux, who paraded around the dressing room three weeks ago with a supportive wrap around his lower back, said he might take off the second of back-to-back games as a prophylaxis. Indeed, he sat out Pittsburgh's 4–3 loss to the

ky's career-points mark—but he might redefine the bloated language of the sport, in which *star* is attached to anyone who scores a point per game.

Lemieux was supposed to have passed the torch, not quietly set fire to the reputation of an entire generation with it. Remember the dreamy TV introduction to the 2000 All-Star Game in Toronto, a filmed segment that showed Lemieux with Gretzky and Gordie Howe walking toward a frozen pond, symbolically ceding the game to Jagr, Eric Lindros, Pavel Bure and Paul Kariya? Well, Jagr brooded until Lemieux returned, Lindros isn't playing, Bure's scoring hasn't ignited the dreadful Florida Panthers, and through Sunday, Kariya was scuffling along with 21 goals for the bedraggled Mighty Ducks.

"Mario picked the torch back up," Minnesota general manager Doug Risebrough says. "What it tells me is that we're in the business to promote our game, and we've probably promoted some people to star status who aren't really stars. They're obviously good players, but they aren't stars in the classic sense. Everybody in the league is trying to have that star so fans can identify with him, and then you get a guy like Lemieux back and you see what a true star is. It might bring a little bit of ammonia to the nostrils of the league."

Lemieux, though, is so good that using him as the standard for stardom may be unrealistic. "Lemieux might be the most talented player ever," says Kariya. Says Lemaire, "He's the only guy who can make the puck disappear for a second. Here's the puck now—oops, where is it? He still has it." Compared with Lemieux's ability to make regular-season apathy vanish, to turn the Penguins into a circus team, to make every Pittsburgh game Christmas morning, his magic with the puck is a mere parlor trick.

The one place Lemieux doesn't stand out is in the Penguins' dressing room, at least no more than he ever did. General manager Craig Patrick has fixed up the place; he has imported some tough guys, like forwards Steve McKenna and Krzysztof Oliwa, traded for Mario allies in Bergevin and the rejuvenated Kevin Stevens, and made the room as homey as it was when Pittsburgh was winning Cups. Bergevin threatens to leap into Lemieux's lap twice a month when paychecks are distributed—"Our Santa," he teases—but Lemieux says he's now 99% player and 1% owner. He calls the office every few days but has been in the executive suite only a couple of times in the past several weeks, once for a morning staff meeting on Jan. 25, hours after he had gotten a hat trick against the Canadiens. As he walked into the boardroom, his executive assistant, Elaine Heufelder, said, "Not too shabby last night, boss." You think anyone ever said that to Chicago Blackhawks owner Bill Wirtz?

The playoffs will diffuse hockey's attention, but for the next month the Mario cam is on 24/7. This is his story, his season, one so remarkable it has ennobled and embarrassed the NHL at the same time. Barring injury, it should only get better. □

Washington Capitals on Saturday, the night after the Rangers game. It was the first time since he returned that he had missed a match.

"You can see he's getting more comfortable, doing things now he wasn't a few weeks ago," Penguins defenseman Darius Kasparaitis says. "He should be in the best shape ever by playoff time. He's becoming the most dangerous player in the league again, maybe more than Jagr."

There's a subtext to Lemieux's surreal comeback, one less flattering to the league. Lemieux, 35, won't rewrite the record books—he's 13 100-point seasons or so behind Gretz-

GREATEST PENGUINS

PAUL COFFEY
D, 1987-92

A smooth skater and prolific scorer as a defenseman, Coffey broke the 100-point barrier twice for Pittsburgh and was key to the Penguins' winning their first Cup.

BRUCE BENNETT STUDIOS/GETTY IMAGES

KEVIN STEVENS
LW, 1987-95

An essential figure on the Penguins' first two title teams, the power forward scored 17 playoff goals in 1991 and had 123 regular-season points in 1991-92.

FRED VUICH

AL TIELEMANS

MARK RECCHI

RW, 1989-92, 2005-06, '06-07

Recchi led the Penguins with 113 points during the 1990-91 regular season and added 34 points in 24 playoff games that year; he averaged nearly a point a game over three Penguins stints.

TOM BARRASSO

G, 1988-2000
One of the best American-born goalies ever, he was between the pipes for two Stanley Cup wins and 226 regular-season victories.

KEN WREGGET

G, 1992-98

The veteran backed up Tom Barrasso, which meant Wregget saw plenty of action with Barrasso's frequent injuries. In 1994-95 Wregget had a record of 25-9-2, and in '96, SI dubbed him "the surprise star of the postseason."

DENIS BRODEUR/NHLI/GETTY IMAGES

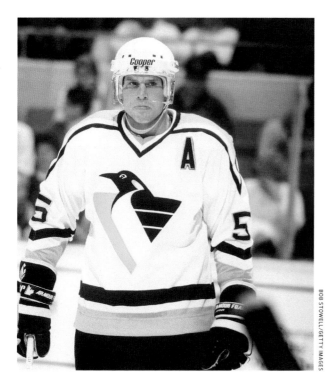

DK SPORTS/GETTY IMAGES

ULF SAMUELSSON

D, 1991-95

The blue-line brute was a defensive power on the 1990s Cup teams, and in the '91 playoffs he delivered a body check on Boston's Cam Neely so nasty that it shortened the Bruin's career.

BOB STOWELL/GETTY IMAGES

GREATEST PENGUINS

LARRY MURPHY
D, 1990-95

Murphy and his wicked slap shot were essential to the winning formula, in Pittsburgh and beyond; after lifting two Cups as a Penguin, he took another two in the 1990s as a Red Wing.

JOE MULLEN
RW, 1990-95,'96-97

A two-time All-Star before he arrived in Pittsburgh, the vet was a consistent scorer on the loaded Cup teams, and as a Penguin he made his third career All-Star team with 70 points in 1993-94.

JOHN BIEVER

BRUCE BENNETT STUDIOS/GETTY IMAGES

BOB JOHNSON

After coaching Pittsburgh to its first Stanley Cup, the relentlessly positive Badger Bob was stricken with brain cancer

BY JAY GREENBERG

FROM SPORTS ILLUSTRATED
OCTOBER 21, 1991

BOB JOHNSON has trouble speaking, but no trouble believing. Johnson is largely paralyzed on his left side, but he can write with his right hand and see his team play on television, via satellite dish, in his Colorado Springs home. Therefore he can still be Badger Bob, which means living each day for hockey, just as he did before he underwent surgery in August for brain cancer.

So after the Penguins beat the Flyers 6–3 recently in Philadelphia, Pittsburgh assistant coach Barry Smith asked directions to the nearest phone. Smith had promised to call Johnson following the game and fill him in on whatever he couldn't see on television. After each of Pittsburgh's four games so far this season Johnson was faxed the game evaluations of the players, and when he felt up to it, he sent interim coach Scotty Bowman suggestions for attacking the next opponent. "This team keeps him going," said Smith as he hurried down the hallway. "It gives him a focus."

Johnson's wife, Martha, fields the phone calls. She was thrilled that her husband was able to come home from the hospital last week. Of course, neither she nor the Penguins, who have delayed raising their 1991 Stanley Cup championship banner until Johnson can travel to see it, need a medical opinion to believe that he is going to bounce back. Last year he taught his team how.

Johnson won three NCAA titles in 15 seasons at Wisconsin, taking a year out to coach the 1976 U.S. Olympic team, before leaving in '82 to become coach of the Calgary Flames, whom he lifted from mediocrity to the NHL's upper echelon. He left the Flames in '87, two seasons before they won the Cup, because he felt the executive directorship of USA Hockey, the head administrative position for hockey in the U.S., was something he could not turn down. But he soon learned that he was a coach, not an administrator, and in June '90

the perfect team for Johnson—talented but with a poor self-image—lured him to Pittsburgh.

"I thought, This guy can't be for real," said defenseman Paul Coffey. "Nobody can be that up all the time. But he made us believers." In particular, he made them believers in the playoffs, during which the Penguins fell behind in all four series before pulling out victory—just as Johnson told them they could.

"I've reached the top of the mountain," he said after the Penguins smashed the Minnesota North Stars 8–0 to win the Cup four games to two. Typically, he paused only briefly before ascending toward the next peak. Johnson, 60, agreed to coach the U.S. Canada Cup team for a fourth time.

But as the American players reported to Pittsburgh for the opening of Team USA's training camp in August, Johnson became aware that his speech was slightly slurred. He suspected a dental ailment and coached the team on a 12-day exhibition tour. Those closest to him noticed the slurring too, and they saw that he was also having mild coordination problems in eating and that he looked tired.

When the U.S. team returned to Pittsburgh two days before its Aug. 31 tournament opener, Johnson arranged to undergo medical tests. But that evening his condition dramatically worsened. Emergency surgery was performed hours later to remove a bleeding, life-threatening tumor on the right side of his brain. Another tumor was inoperable.

The news shook the sport. Who in the hockey community had not been touched by Johnson? When Jaromir Jagr, who didn't know enough English as an 18-year-old Penguin rookie last season to carry on a simple conversation with his coach, was told at the Czechoslovakian team's training camp in Saskatoon, Saskatchewan, of Johnson's plight, he broke down and cried.

The American players, most of whom had learned the gospel of hockey from Johnson at a clinic or a school somewhere in their youth, were stunned. "I never thought anything would go wrong with Badger," said Team USA and Calgary

Flames defenseman Gary Suter.

As is his nature, Johnson didn't get down in the dumps about his condition. The day following the surgery, he wrote memos to his stand-in coach, Tim Taylor. Before the Americans played their semifinal game against Finland, Johnson faxed the team this message: "For all the kids in the border towns from Minnesota to New York, you are their heroes. All the hockey kids idolize [Wayne] Gretzky. I want them to idolize players like [Jeremy] Roenick and [Mike] Modano from the U.S. USA Hockey needs identity. This is our chance to reach out for some."

The Americans made the finals but lost to Canada. By then, Johnson had been transferred to the hospital in Colorado Springs. "The fire of coaching still burns inside me," he said as he left Pittsburgh. "When I return, it will be my greatest day in coaching."

COACH, 1990-91

The beloved Badger Bob, so named for his success at the University of Wisconsin, where his teams took three NCAA titles, won a Stanley Cup in his only season on the Pittsburgh bench.

The Penguins know to hope for something more realistic than Johnson's coming back to their bench. "I just want him to be able to enjoy his life again," says Penguins defenseman Ulf Samuelsson. During last season's playoffs, Johnson leaned on Bowman, the Penguins' player personnel director, for advice. Now Bowman is asking for help.

The Penguins' championship rings arrived from the manufacturer last week. General manager Craig Patrick arranged to get Johnson's ring early and flew to Colorado Springs with it. Like other members of the Penguins organization, Patrick has difficulty accepting Johnson's illness. "I think I'm still in the denial stage," he said in his office last week as tears ran down his cheeks. "I'm still very hopeful that Bob is going to be back."

Johnson taught the Penguins to think as he does, so they are leaving a light on for him.   □

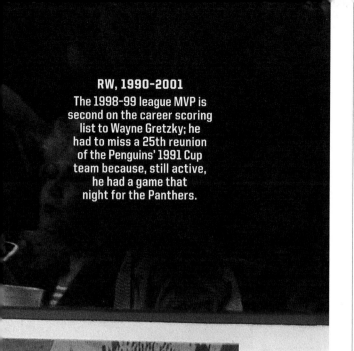

RW, 1990-2001

The 1998-99 league MVP is second on the career scoring list to Wayne Gretzky; he had to miss a 25th reunion of the Penguins' 1991 Cup team because, still active, he had a game that night for the Panthers.

JAROMIR JAGR

The Czech star grew up loving America but needed time to feel at home in Pittsburgh

BY E.M. SWIFT

FROM SPORTS ILLUSTRATED
OCTOBER 12, 1992

WHEN JAROMIR JAGR was 12 years old—long before he was a shaggy-maned, spotlight-nabbing heartthrob of the Pittsburgh Penguins; heck, before he had ever left Kladno, Czechoslovakia—he kept a certain photograph in his grade book at school. Jagr had cut it out of a magazine and hidden it there, sneaking peeks at the picture, knowing there would be hell to pay if the teacher caught him with it.

One day, sure enough, the teacher picked up Jagr's grade book to write down the score he had made on a test and found the photograph. Are you crazy, Jaromir? Take it out, she told him. So he did. But as soon as class was over, Jagr put the photograph of Ronald Reagan, president of the United States, back into his grade book. Jagr admired Reagan because he was somebody who stood up to the Communists, who had identified the Soviet Union as the "evil empire" that Jagr's family knew it to be.

"In school we were always taught the Soviet doctrine," Jagr says. "The U.S.A. was bad and wanted war. Russia was our friend and was preventing the United States from bombing us. Even my father didn't tell me the truth, because he was afraid I'd say something in school that would get us into trouble. But my grandmother, she told me the truth."

Jagr's grandmother Jarmila told the boy about the first Jaromir Jagr, his grandfather and her husband. He was a farmer. When the Communists took over Czechoslovakia in

1948, the grandmother said, they appropriated all the privately owned farms. They collectivized his grandfather's fields and three-quarters of his livestock. They left him with the house, barn and yard that the family still lives in today—Jagr, his grandmother, his parents and his uncle. Then the authorities told Jagr's grandfather that he had to labor in the cooperative farm for free. His grandfather refused to work for those people who had stolen his farm. So he was thrown into jail, and he remained there for more than two years.

Jaromir Jagr, the hockey player, never knew Jaromir Jagr, the farmer. The grandson was born in 1972. The grandfather died in 1968, by coincidence during the glorious days of the Czechoslovakian freedom movement known as the Prague Spring. "He never knew that the Russians came back," Jagr says. But, of course, they did come back, and Jagr's grandmother made sure that he knew how, on Aug. 20–21, 1968, the troops rolled through Czechoslovakia to squash that fledgling movement in less than 48 hours.

Jagr never forgot. That is why he admired Reagan. And why the young Penguins star, the flamboyant and seemingly carefree spirit, handsome, athletic and rich, wears number 68, after the Prague Spring of 1968, the spring that his grandfather died.

Czechoslovakia's revolution of 1989 enabled Jagr to fulfill his lifelong dream of playing in the NHL without having to defect. When the Penguins made Jagr their first draft choice in June 1990, the fifth player taken overall, he was in Vancouver for the proceedings, the first time a Czechoslovakian player had attended the NHL draft with his government's blessings.

His rookie season in Pittsburgh was harder than he had imagined. The Penguins set him up with an English tutor and found a Czechoslovakian family in Pittsburgh he could live with. But as the season progressed, Jagr grew increasingly miserable. He missed his family and friends. He never went out. All he had was hockey, and verbal communication was so limited between Jagr and the coaching staff that when the coaches tried to explain to him the rule about the maximum curve allowed on a stick, Jagr thought they were yelling at him again for not shooting enough.

On Dec. 13, recognizing his young star was "slipping farther and farther away," Patrick made a deal with Calgary for a veteran Czechoslovakian player, Jiri Hrdina. "Jags was really down low when I got there," recalls Hrdina, who is back with the Flames now as a scout. "He wasn't going to go home or anything, but he felt alone."

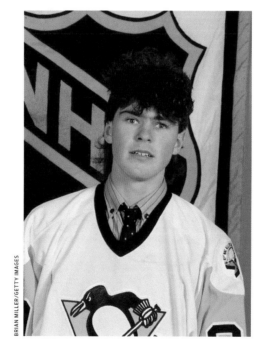

BRIAN MILLER/GETTY IMAGES

STEVE BABINEAU/NHL/GETTY IMAGES

MULLET OVER
Jagr, 18 years old at the 1990 NHL Draft (above), led the league in scoring five times as a Penguin.

Jagr responded with a strong second half, scoring 37 of his 57 points in the last 40 games of the season. In the 1991 playoffs he led all rookies in scoring, with three goals and 10 assists. Nice numbers, to be sure, but no one was putting Jagr's name in the same sentence with Mario Lemieux's.

That all changed last season. More comfortable with the language and more confident with his talent, Jagr played with such flair that someone figured out that Jaromir was an anagram for Mario Jr. His regular-season totals—32 goals and 37 assists in 70 games—weren't nearly as spectacular on paper as they appeared in the flesh. Screaming down the right wing, his long dark hair flopping behind his helmet, the lefthanded-shooting Jagr would time and again beat both defensemen like a pair of rented mules.

Bowman's difficulty last season was finding Jagr enough ice time. The Penguins started the season overloaded at right wing, with Joe Mullen, a former 50-goal scorer, and Mark Recchi, who scored 40 goals in '90–91, in addition to Jagr. "Jagr really got shortchanged on the power play," Bowman admits. Only four of Jagr's 32 goals came with a man advantage. "It got to be a problem. He would come to me, very upset. 'I don't play here next year. Too many stars here. I got agent of Brett Hull and Wayne Gretzky. I go to San Jose. I be a star.' That's one of the reasons we traded Recchi."

With Recchi dealt to Philadelphia late in the season and Mullen injured, Jagr's ice time increased dramatically in the playoffs. If it hadn't, it's doubtful the Penguins would have repeated as Stanley Cup champs. When Lemieux had his left hand slashed and broken by Adam Graves of the Rangers in the divisional finals, Jagr simply took over for his hockey idol. In Game 5, with the series 2–2, Jagr scored on a penalty shot, then won the game with five minutes left by undressing defenseman Jeff Beukeboom before tallying the game-winner. Jagr finished off the Rangers in Game 6, again scoring the game-winning goal, and followed that by scoring in overtime against the Bruins in the first game of the conference finals.

In style Jagr is something much different from Lemieux. "When Mario gets the puck, he's always thinking, Where can I put it?" says Bowman. "He'll pass the puck off and get himself in a better situation to score than he was in. When Jaromir gets the puck, he's always thinking, Where can I go with it? He reminds me of Maurice Richard in that way."

"I just play," Jagr says. He doesn't even like to know the name of the defenseman he is going against. "If I see Chris Chelios is there, I think, I can't beat him. And I won't beat him. Better I don't notice. When you go one-on-one with good defenseman, you do same things as against bad defenseman. Sometimes, you get lucky." ☐

RON FRANCIS

His accomplishments were overshadowed by those of more celebrated Penguins, but he handled it with a humility he learned early in life

BY GERRY CALLAHAN

FROM SPORTS ILLUSTRATED
MARCH 23, 1998

WHEN HE arrived in the NHL, straight out of Junior A at age 18, Ron Francis was barely old enough to shave, a fact that somehow escaped the notice of his new teammates. Shortly after Francis joined the Hartford Whalers in November 1981, a group of veterans tied him to a trainer's table, blindfolded him and introduced him to the joys of the full-body shave. While it surely would have helped if the guys had used shaving cream or at least a little warm water, Francis still looks back fondly on his painful initiation into the NHL. "That's how long I've been around," says Francis, smiling. "Back then, rookies got shaved. That doesn't happen much anymore."

At least it doesn't happen much in Pittsburgh, where Francis wears the C with the same class and dignity that has marked his 17 years in the league. In a game that often eats its best citizens alive, Francis has quietly slipped through the cracks and into the record books.

Not that Francis expects anyone to notice. He played the first 9½ years of his career in Hartford, the NHL's version of the witness protection program, and the next seven with the Penguins in the prodigious shadows of Mario Lemieux and Jaromir Jagr. While his spectacular teammates have won the awards, Francis settled for the respect of his peers, and few players in the game can match him in that category. "The ultimate professional," Pittsburgh goaltender Tom Barrasso says of Francis. "He doesn't make the big headlines, doesn't get the big contract. He's just a very special player who has quietly become one of the all-time greats."

Francis would appear to be a lock for the Hall of Fame, but you will have to forgive him if he waits until all the ballots are counted before he takes a bow. Despite his obvious qualifications, it's hard for Francis to believe he will get into the Hall when he can't even get on the All-Star Game ballot. This season's ballot for the North American team listed the names of 12 centers, but the 6' 3", 200-pound Francis wasn't among them. "I'll admit that bothered me a little," he says. "But a couple of years ago, I was third in the league in scoring and didn't get voted to the All-Star team. I was added later as the commissioner's choice."

Before the ballot snub, there was the little matter of the Canadian Olympic team slight, another elite club for which Francis wasn't selected. Of those chosen, only Wayne Gretzky is ahead of Francis on the NHL's career scoring list. In typical Francis fashion, he says he felt worse for Mark Messier than for himself. "How can you not have Mess on that team after all he's done?" says Francis.

When Kevin Constantine was hired to coach Pittsburgh last June, he brought with him a new system, a more disciplined, defense-oriented style of play that required the commitment of the veterans, especially the first-line center. Constantine and Francis spoke on the phone many times over the summer, and the latter assured the former that he was ready to buy into everything Constantine was selling. With Francis on board, Jagr and the rest of the team fell in line. "From Day One we were counting on Ronnie," says Constantine. "He hasn't disappointed."

Francis believes his performance this year is largely the result of a new diet, which is higher in protein and lower in starch, as well as an intense stretching regimen. Francis's greatest asset remains his understanding of the game and his vision on the ice. "Maybe I've lost some strength," he says, "but my mind is the best part of my game, and as far as I know, I haven't lost my mind yet."

While ordering lunch, Francis tells the waitress to hold the french fries, and he is asked if that's a concession to his new regimen. "Actually, no," he says. "I gave them up for Lent." He can be as dull as Sunday school but at the same time

refreshing: a religious man who doesn't beat you over the head with his beliefs, a family man who doesn't wave his three children in front of the cameras like props.

He's asked how he tolerates life in the shadows, always watching quietly while someone else gets the attention, and he reluctantly reveals his secret—he's had lots of practice. Ricky Francis is two years younger than brother Ron and is mentally retarded. As a child, Ricky suffered seizures, sometimes as many as 25 in a day, and Ron helped his parents, Lorita and Ron, care for his brother, often joining them on late-night trips to the hospital. "When Ricky was nine, doctors told my parents to put him in an institution, that he'd be dead within three years," says Ron. "They refused, and he's still living with them. That was 24 years ago."

With advances in medication, Ricky rarely suffers seizures

C, 1991-98
The two-time team captain had two 100-point seasons and two 90-point seasons, was named the NHL's best defensive forward in 1995 and won the Lady Bing Memorial Trophy twice.

and works at a furniture store near his family's home in Sault Ste. Marie, Ont. He's also a talented cross-country skier who's a Special Olympics world champion in the 7.5 km and 10 km.

When Ricky was competing in the Special Olympics World Winter Games in Canada in February 1997, the Penguins gave Ron permission to fly to Toronto during the season to watch Ricky race. Ron saw Ricky win the 10 km and presented him with one of his two golds. The elder Ron says it was like "watching Ricky win his own Stanley Cup." To Ron, draping the medal around his brother's neck was more memorable than holding the Cup. "Just looking at his face made me realize what's important," he says.

Just looking at Ron Francis's face makes you realize why he didn't make a big deal out of his Olympic snub: His kid brother won enough gold for both of them. □

SCOTTY BOWMAN

The coach added to his Cup total and softened his manner when he took over for the late Bob Johnson

BY E.M. SWIFT

FROM SPORTS ILLUSTRATED
MAY 10, 1993

A BRUPT, STRAIGHTFORWARD, *without flair or charm, he seems cold and abrasive, sometimes obnoxious, controversial but never colorful. He is not Vince Lombardi, tough and gruff with a heart of gold. His players don't sit around telling hateful-affectionate stories about him. . . . He is complex, confusing, misunderstood, unclear in every way but one. He is a brilliant coach, the best of his time.*
—KEN DRYDEN, *The Game*, 1983

The players are different now. And I found out you can do things differently. —SCOTTY BOWMAN, 1993

This story might have been subtitled "The mellowing of hockey's winningest coach." Might have been if William Scott Bowman had cooperated and mellowed to any appreciable degree. He hasn't. Oh, he has smoothed out some of the renowned rough edges he featured in the 1960s, when as a young up-and-comer he cajoled and browbeat the expansion St. Louis Blues into overachieving their way into three straight Stanley Cup finals.

He has tempered the unpredictable, intimidating style he used in the '70s, when, chin distinctively thrust out, he drove the firewagon-style Montreal Canadiens to five Stanley Cups in eight years. But you wouldn't say the coach of the Stanley Cup champion Pittsburgh Penguins has mellowed.

Any temptation to think so is laid to rest by a chance meeting with a taxi driver who regularly services the downtown hotel in Pittsburgh that Bowman calls home during the hockey season. "I almost got in a fight with him last year," says the

cabbie, some 30 years Bowman's junior. "I was parked where he couldn't get past me in the garage, and he wasn't any too subtle telling me to move. He's definitely got an attitude. I finally told him to relax or he was going to have a heart attack."

Bowman traces his competitiveness to his 86-year-old mother, Jean, who to this day will throw her cards in the fire if she loses at euchre. "If you like the game, Scott, why lose at it?" she once said to him, and that advice would look good as his epitaph.

Bowman, the second-oldest of four children, grew up in Verdun, a working-class suburb of Montreal. His parents were Scottish immigrants, and if he learned competitiveness from his mother, Bowman learned the value of hard work from his father, who in 31 years of pounding sheet metal for the railway never took a sick day.

As a lad Bowman could strap on his blades in front of his apartment and skate down snow-covered 5th Avenue, through the back alleys, to the city rinks where he learned to play hockey. Verdun had dozens of rinks. By March 1951 Bowman was a pro prospect. He was 17 years old, a small, quick, talented forward for the respected Junior Canadiens. Then, almost as soon as his playing career had started, it was over. In the final minutes of a Junior A playoff game at the Montreal Forum, Bowman broke in alone on goal, chased by a defenseman named Jean-Guy Talbot, whose team, Trois-Rivières, was on the verge of being eliminated. Out of pure frustration Talbot swung his stick at Bowman once, twice, striking him in the shoulder and then the head. Bowman, like every player back then, wasn't wearing a helmet. He went down like a tree. "Scott put his hand up," Jean Bowman recalled not long ago, "and a piece of his skull came off his head."

"It was like being scalped," Bowman says.

Talbot was suspended from hockey for a year, a suspension that was lifted eight months later. He went on to play 17 years in the NHL. Bowman, his skull fractured, hung up his blades at 18.

Did he ever forgive Talbot? Did he ever speak to the so-and-so again? "It was in the heat of the game, eh?" Bowman says matter-of-factly. "He just totally lost it. It was his fifth penalty of the game. We picked him up on waivers, and he played for me three years in St. Louis."

Classic Bowman. He doesn't hold grudges. Grudges can't help you win hockey games. But he learned something he would always remember, a motivational tool he would em-

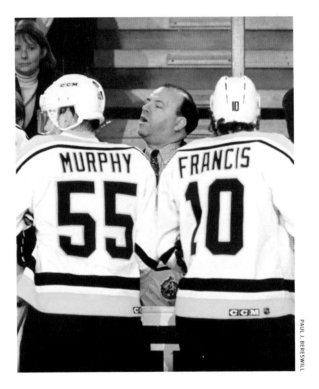

PAUL J. BERESWILL

ploy throughout his coaching career. There is no greater punishment a coach can inflict on a hockey player than to not let him play.

His playing career over, Bowman turned to coaching. First 12-and 13-year-olds, then 14 and 15. By the time he was 22, Bowman was coaching 20-year-olds at the Junior B level. It paid him $250 a year, so to make a living he took a job at a paint company five minutes from the Forum. Every day he took an early lunch, 11 a.m. to noon, so he could walk down and watch Dick Irvin's Canadiens practice.

Irvin used to say that if you could get your team to laugh before a big game, you had an edge. Bowman watched, learned, absorbed. People noticed him, marveled at how Bowman commanded respect from players nearly his own age. In 1956 the Junior Canadiens moved from Montreal to Ottawa, and the team's coach and general manager, Sam Pollock, asked the 23-year-old Bowman to be his assistant. "Pollock was a very demanding coach," says Bowman. "His philosophy was, You go with your best players as much as you can. I learned that from him."

After the team won the 1958 Memorial Cup, the top prize in junior hockey, Bowman took over his own Junior A team in Peterborough, Ont. He coached there for three seasons, then became the Montreal Canadiens' head scout for eastern Canada. But he missed coaching and moved back behind the bench of the Junior Canadiens in '63–64.

It was then that he met Montreal's Toe Blake, the coach of eight Cup winners. "I used to go into his office a lot," says Bowman. "And he might say something like, 'I'll let you in on a tip. Your friend Terry Harper's not going to play much tonight.' He knew how each of his players did against everyone else. Certain guys do well against one team but not another. He was a good strategist and a good matchup man and wasn't afraid to sit guys out to change his ammunition."

When Bowman's Junior Canadiens were matched up against a superior opponent in the playoffs, Blake called him in and drew up three radically different forechecking schemes for Bowman to try. All of them worked, and Bowman learned another lesson: If you threw something different at a team, almost anything, it got the players out of rhythm, slowed them down, kept them off balance. No matter how clever the opposing coach was, it took his team some time to react to the changes. And by that time Bowman, always a step ahead, might have altered his strategy again. It was a good way to play when you were outmanned. "I found out that if you're going to win games, you had better be ready to adapt," he says.

In 1990, Bowman had been an analyst for *Hockey Night in Canada* when Patrick offered him the job as the Penguins' director of player personnel, and Bowman jumped at it. It was a good fit for everyone. Bowman, whose last job had been with the Sabres, could remain in Buffalo with his family, scout teams for Bob Johnson, then the Penguin coach, and occasionally commute to Pittsburgh for consultations.

As a coach Badger Bob was as different from Bowman in style as one could imagine—garrulous, cheerful, an incessant communicator, nonconfrontational, paternal. But they shared a deep mutual respect. After watching Mario Lemieux get shadowed one game, Bowman made a suggestion to Johnson: Tell Mario to pick up an opposing player on the ice when he's being shadowed, so he'll have two guys on him. It was a tactic Bowman sometimes had used with in Montreal with Guy Lafleur. Johnson liked the idea but asked Bowman to present it to Mario himself. "He made me feel I was part of the coaching staff, and I wasn't," Bowman says.

The Penguins were a relaxed outfit under Johnson and, led by the unstoppable Lemieux, went on to win the 1991 Stanley Cup. That summer the hockey world was stunned when Johnson was stricken with brain cancer. Patrick appointed Bowman, who had traveled with the team throughout the playoffs, the interim coach. "It wasn't like Craig said, 'Come in and coach for the year,'" Bowman recalls. "It was, 'Keep the job until Bob comes back.' We hung on to the hope that a miracle would happen. But a month into the season, we knew he wasn't coming back."

Johnson died in November 1991, and Patrick, believing the team had gone through enough changes, asked Bowman to finish the year. The Penguins didn't play as soundly on defense as he liked, but Bowman was reluctant to tamper too much with a style that had won them the Cup. There was also the matter of changing his temperament. "I was aware that if I coached the way I did in the past," Bowman says, "it wouldn't have brought the same results. I knew I had to be different. If you're critical of a player today, especially openly, it's perceived as being negative. Bob Johnson was so positive. You have to stroke them more."

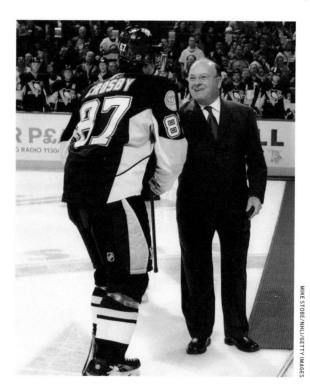

PAST & PRESENT
Bowman, then retired, met Sidney Crosby before a game at Nassau Coliseum in November 2007.

MIKE STOBE/NHL/GETTY IMAGES

Bowman chose not to run the Penguins' practices, delegating that responsibility to Johnson's—now his—assistants, Barry Smith and Rick Kehoe. He kept a wary distance from the team, and the team muddled along with a 39-32-9 regular-season record. "Scotty, especially at first, was not as available as Badger," says Lemieux. "He's changed a lot since then. He's become a little closer to the players. With the type of team we have, it's important for the coach to be close."

The turning point may have come in the opening round of the 1992 playoffs, after the Penguins fell behind the Washington Capitals three games to one. Pittsburgh had been unable to control the Capitals' offense, particularly the role Washington's defensemen played in the offense. Lemieux, of all people, came up with a defensive plan. "He came to me the morning of the fifth game and said, 'Why don't we surprise them and play the game close to the vest. Tight, tight, tight,'" Bowman recalls. "I'd never pushed a lot of defensive hockey on this team, but since it was Mario who suggested it...."

They cooked up a forechecking system called the 1–4 delay, in which the Penguins didn't chase the puck in the offensive zone but stacked the neutral zone with players and thought of the blue line as a battleground. It was remarkably similar to one of the forechecking systems Blake had drawn up for Bowman 30 years earlier, when he was coaching the Junior Canadiens. At the Penguins' morning meeting, it was introduced to the rest of the team. Kehoe started to explain it, when Bowman interrupted.

"Fellas, this idea came from Mario," he said. Then he asked Lemieux to explain the 1–4 delay. "Go ahead, Mario."

Lemieux, embarrassed, said no, thank you, that Kehoe was doing just fine. "The team laughed," Bowman remembers. "They got a big kick out of that." He also remembered what Irvin had said so many years before: If you could get your team to laugh before a big game, it gave you an edge. The Penguins, of course, swept the next three games to eliminate the Caps. They then defeated the Rangers, who had been the NHL's top team in the regular season; then the Bruins; and then the Blackhawks, reeling off 11 straight playoff wins, en route to their second—and his sixth—Stanley Cup. Says Bowman, "As great as our teams were in Montreal, we never won 11 straight. We got on a roll and never looked back." □

RW, 1998-2003, '11
The much-traveled right wing had his best statistical seasons as a Penguin, with career highs of 44 goals and 95 points in 2000-01.

ALEXEI KOVALEV

To watch this sublime stickhandler
in action was to see
a brilliant artist at work

BY MICHAEL FARBER

FROM SPORTS ILLUSTRATED
DECEMBER 23, 2002

THIS QUESTION was asked of Pittsburgh Penguins players: If Mario Lemieux and Alexei Kovalev were airlifted to a frozen pond in northern Ontario, given sticks and a puck and asked to do the most spectacular hockey tricks imaginable, who would win—Mario the Magician or the Sorcerer's Apprentice?

There were wows and hedges and political calculations ("He signs my checks," fourth-line wing Steve McKenna said of Lemieux, who also owns the team), and in the end the vote was too close to call. Lemieux has spent his career undressing the NHL's best defensemen with his savvy and slickness. But can he drop to his knees just inside the blue line and saucer the puck 40 feet in the air so it lands on top of the net? Can he, at full speed, put a skate atop the puck, pirouette almost 360 degrees and kick the puck ahead to himself? Kovalev, a right wing, does both of those things.

The swing vote came from an unexpected precinct. "I'd say Kovy," Lemieux admitted. "He's the best stickhandler I've ever seen. Quickness. Hands. A much better stickhandler than me. He's got the talent to be the best player in the world."

Kovalev's game is all curlicues and grace notes: rococo art in an age of dump-in simplicity. He doesn't play hockey, he ornaments it. There are eight million stories of his virtuosity in the naked dressing room, but a favorite is the hat trick he completed against the New York Islanders last season by bursting down the wing, shooting off his back foot as he crossed the goal line and beating Garth Snow high to the short side from a wicked angle—a shot that drew a stare from Snow and a laugh from Kovalev. He raised the bar, then roofed the puck under it.

"How do painters come up with ideas?" Kovalev asked rhetorically as he picked at a chicken Caesar salad one recent afternoon. "Maybe something comes into their heads, and they think about it, and that's what they end up painting. Same thing with me. Something comes into my head, and I'll try it. It looks funny and unreal at first, but then you keep doing it, and it becomes easier."

Kovalev is 6' 1" and 221 pounds of hockey inventiveness, the perfect marriage of man, stick and puck. "He's one of those guys you watch even when he's on the ice by himself," Penguins defenseman Jamie Pushor says. "You can watch a guy shoot hoops alone, but you generally wouldn't watch a hockey player. Except him."

The background: an indifferent crowd on a November night in Sunrise, Fla. The foreground: the Pittsburgh line of Kovalev, Lemieux and wing Aleksey Morozov. The scene: The three Penguins come out whipping the puck around against the Florida Panthers with such brio that those in charge of the in-house music during stoppages should dispense with the rock and roll and play Sweet Georgia Brown. The only trick Kovalev doesn't pull in the first period is the confetti-in-the-water-bucket move. Three times in one play he beats defenseman Ivan Majesky, who chases him around the left face-off circle like a golden retriever.

But in the second period the masterstrokes turn into finger-painting, a mess of blind passes. This is art for art's sake, not hockey's, and it is the sort of display that has marred Kovalev's audacious work throughout his pro career, which began with the New York Rangers in 1992–93. Lately he has become a superior finisher, and over the past two-plus seasons he has ranked sixth in shots, having overcome an innate Russian reticence about firing the puck. Yet in weak moments he chooses style over substance.

"His game has changed," Penguins defenseman Ian Moran says. "But he still enjoys beating guys one-on-one too much." For instance, against Florida, Kovalev runs out of room along the boards and drops a soft pass to Lemieux that results in a turnover and a four-on-two rush by the Panthers. Kovalev makes almost no effort to get back into the play. He is out of gas at the end of a shift that lasts too long, which recalls an incident years ago that became the signature piece in his portfolio.

Kovalev scored the goal that preceded Mark Messier's famous hat trick in Game 6 of the 1994 semifinals between the

Rangers and the New Jersey Devils; and the next postseason he lay on the ice long enough after getting slashed for the referee to stop play and disallow a Nordiques goal; but the most memorable story about him involves a game against the Boston Bruins in 1994. Kovalev had been overstaying his standard 45-second shift so routinely that in the third period, when he finally skated to the bench for a change, the exasperated Rangers coach, Mike Keenan, waved at him to stay on the ice. This went on and on until the game was over. Depending on whom you believe, Kovalev played a record 11- or nine- or four-minute shift. Keenan has always maintained that until his teammates clued him in following the match, Kovalev thought he was being rewarded rather than punished. Kovalev, however, insists he had it figured out within three minutes.

In Pittsburgh things do not always have to be accomplished in a New York minute. The Eurocentric Penguins have a loose group because management usually allows players to find their own comfort level by letting them be creative on the ice. A liberated Kovalev, who was shipped to Pittsburgh in November 1998 for center Petr Nedved, ultimately became a point-a-game player.

The next big move for the 29-year-old Kovalev could be out of Pittsburgh. He has arbitration rights next season and the presumed bonanza of unrestricted free agency in 2004. Fleeing the artists' colony in Pittsburgh might be lousy for his career—he won't ride shotgun for Lemieux or have the same degree of freedom in another system—but he would undoubtedly become the best-paid freelancer in history.

BOB ROSATO

TOO GOOD
Kovalev's confidence and talent sometimes impelled him to go one-on-one in situations he shouldn't have.

"As players we learn a lot about the game and ourselves as we progress through our careers," says Manderville. "For Alexei it's a much more pronounced education because of his skill. In the final part of last year, with Mario out [with a hip injury], the team relied on Alexei heavily to produce. He did. And he definitely has another level beyond that. Certainly there's a fire in his eyes."

That is either fire or the glimmer of an idea for his next suitable-for-framing star turn. He was watching a tape of his old goals recently and saw a wraparound move in which he came down the left side handling the puck on his forehand and circled the net. He figures that the next time, instead of trying to stuff the puck inside the post, he'll keep going, keep drifting, keep patient and, poof, top-shelf. Coming soon to an 18,000-seat frozen pond near you. □

GREATEST PENGUINS

MARTIN STRAKA

C, 1992-95, '97-2003

The 1992 first-round pick's initial run in Pittsburgh was disappointing, but Straka picked it up on the return trip, with 83 points in '98-99 and a career-best 95 points in 2000-01.

MARC-ANDRE FLEURY

Changes in pad color and in puckhandling technique helped a young goalie develop into an enduring figure between the pipes

BY MICHAEL FARBER

FROM SPORTS ILLUSTRATED
MAY 19, 2008

EXTREME MAKEOVER, NHL Edition: Marc-André Fleury's transformation began last autumn in the Ottawa home of Janet Leduc. Although a committed Senators fan, Leduc is foremost an optometrist. (As you are no doubt aware, there is no eye in team.) After being driven to distraction for years while watching Fleury flash his trademark taxicab-yellow pads on TV, Leduc permitted professional judgment to supersede hometown loyalty and said enough was enough. In November, Leduc sent letters to the Penguins' owners, coaches and general manager Ray Shero, explaining that yellow is the color most easily distinguished by the human eye—a nifty graph was enclosed—and recommended that their goalie switch to white pads to better blend with the ice and end boards. As Leduc said by telephone recently, "If there were a sniper walking around, I wouldn't be dressing in yellow. It's too visible. That's why the Golden Arches are yellow, why school buses are yellow." Shero passed on his copy of the letter to head athletic trainer Chris Stewart, who, in December, showed it to Fleury.

The missive arrived at the ideal time. "I was bored," Fleury says. Instead of getting a tattoo or pink highlights like other bored people his age, Fleury, 23, then early in what would be an almost three-month rehabilitation for a high-ankle sprain, decided to request a set of pads in white, with only a sliver of Penguins gold. When Fleury made his first rehab start with the Penguins' AHL affiliate in Wilkes-Barre, his legs were draped in virginal Reebok white. After he stopped 30 of 31 shots to get the win, he was sold on his new look, although he hedged by traveling the minors with his old yellers. Dressed in the white pads when he returned to the NHL in late February—they did make him look bigger, his Penguins teammates agreed—Fleury had a .947 save percentage, yielded an average of 1.53 goals per game and won 10 of 13 starts over the rest of the regular season, then prevailed in 10 of his first 11 in the playoffs after a 4—2 win in Game 2 on Sunday.

So, Dr. Leduc, we get the stuff about white making it difficult for shooters to distinguish a goalie's pads in traffic, but can you explain why wearing it also makes you a better puckhandler?

Seven minutes into the first period of hockey's Pennsylvania primary, Flyers forward Mike Knuble was bearing down on the puck just to the left and rear of the Pittsburgh crease. Fleury took two strides behind the net, corralled the puck, looked off the intruder and then switched to his backhand, rimming a 10-footer to a defenseman to start a Pittsburgh breakout. For a puck-moving maestro like, say, the Dallas Stars' Marty Turco, this pass would have fallen at the midpoint of the spectrum between ho and hum, but for Fleury, who used to treat the puck as if it had cooties, his élan in making the play was wondrous.

Ignore for a moment the cosmetic pad change. The essence of this makeover is the guts of Fleury's game, which has evolved dramatically since he returned from his ankle injury. "It's almost like two different goalies the way he's playing now," Pittsburgh defenseman Sergei Gonchar says. "He's much more comfortable." The difference is as stark as black and, well, you know.

Fleury has always has been a dervish in net, boasting hockey's quickest legs when he entered the NHL in 2003–04. In the crease he was like a duck whose legs were paddling furiously beneath the water's surface, churning constantly and often uselessly. Fleury is still nimble—midway through the second period of Game 1 he read a tricky bounce and butterflied swiftly to make a pad save on an attempted stuff-in by Philadelphia's R.J. Umberger—but now he rarely takes himself out of position to make a stop.

If Fleury now makes saves by letting the puck come to him, he also has started going to the puck when he has an opportunity to play it with his stick. You've heard of stay-at-home defensemen? Fleury was a stay-at-home goalie. In the five-game thrashing that Ottawa gave the Penguins

After so many years as the
Penguins' top goalie,
the two-time All-Star has his
name all over the
franchise record book.

DAVE SANDFORD/NHLI/GETTY IMAGES

in the first round of last year's playoffs, Fleury looked like he was tethered to his net. He was making his defensemen vulnerable by not intercepting pucks and thus not relieving the pressure from the Senators' furious forecheck. Ottawa would angle dump-ins to the corner to Fleury's right, obliging the gaggle of Pittsburgh defensemen with lefthanded shots to play the puck on their backhands while being mashed into the glass. Fleury was mostly a bystander to the carnage, although hardly innocent.

But as they might say in the optometry business, there was more to Fleury's reticence in handling the puck than meets the eye. There was a sad, almost secret backstory. Late in the 2004 World Junior Championships final against the U.S., Fleury came out to pokecheck Patrick O'Sullivan, who was hurtling in on a breakaway. The goalie played the puck, but it struck teammate Braydon Coburn in the back of the leg and caromed into the net for the Americans' winning goal, a Bucknerian moment in Canadian junior hockey history. As Fleury sat shirtless in a trainer's room earlier this postseason,

his omnipresent smile dimmed. "I just didn't want to make mistakes anymore after that [goal]," he said. "I decided I would just focus on stopping [the puck], not worry about making plays; I didn't want to mess up again."

Forget Dr. Leduc. Paging Dr. Freud.

Fleury needed time, and coaching, to heal the pain. Gilles Meloche, a Penguins scout and goalie consultant, has drilled Fleury on the nuances of the position and injected more poise. And, blessedly, backup netminder Ty Conklin is a capable puck mover. Fleury improved during his injury hiatus simply by observing Conklin and pestering him for tips.

After Meloche instructed Fleury to move three feet closer to the goal when the opposing team crossed the red line, the goalie also found the time to go behind the net to settle the puck or move it to a forward. "Now I have an extra second to pick my head up, look and make a play," Fleury said. "Before it was play it right away and hurry back to my net." With this element added to his recommitment to the pokecheck—"Like a boxer. Jabbing, you know?" he said after aborting an Umberger breakaway with his quick stick in Game 1—Fleury has metamorphosed from a twitchy, inconsistent goalie into a dependable netminder, Pittsburgh's white knight. ▫

EVGENI MALKIN

When Sidney Crosby was out with an injury, another Penguin got the opportunity to show the world that he wasn't too shabby himself

BY MICHAEL FARBER

FROM SPORTS ILLUSTRATED
MARCH 5, 2012

RUSSIAN PROVERB Number 1: *Bol'shoi sekret—znaet ves' svet. (Big secret—all the world knows.)*

Evgeni Malkin wraps the blade of his Easton EQ SS stick with white tape, a color preference he shares with maybe 20% of NHL players. But technique, not hue, differentiates a Malkin tape job: He starts at the toe and works backward. A Malkin-izing should be relatively easy to recognize for a practiced eye because the spot where he rips the tape upon completion—literally, the tail of the tape—is at the heel and not the toe. These nuances are noteworthy only because a punk'd Sidney Crosby, a staunch black-tape guy, should have been able to identify the unknown prankster (well, unknown until now) who wrapped his sticks a telltale white when the injured Penguins captain was with the team in November in San Jose.

There is an even more obvious Malkin calling card, one the 6' 3", 195-pound center drops around NHL arenas the way the Lone Ranger once left a silver bullet. He will slip the puck inside the isosceles triangle formed by the defender's stick and skates, unsettling an opponent who has been instructed to take away Malkin's space but who now finds that Malkin has invaded his space. Malkin gains leverage. Then he leans like a skier at a slalom gate, stickhandles and whoosh! He is a conjurer who has created the illusion he has gone through a defender rather than around him.

"Those are incredible displays of hand-puck skills, much to the chagrin of his coach," said Dan Bylsma, who actually is his coach, as he sat in a Boston hotel lobby last month. "Coming out of the [defensive] zone, he'll go underneath a guy's stick three, four times a game, into the triangle. Sometimes he looks like he's doing it for pleasure. Just because he can, you know? Everybody in the world would think it's a bad move, but he's done it 18 times in the last five games, and it's gone wrong once. Kinda tough for me to say, 'No, don't do it.' "

Bylsma worries about Malkin although, in truth, the consternation is directed inward rather than at his player. Bylsma wonders if he bores him. He senses Malkin always knows what he is going to say on the bench or in meetings, just like the center already knows what a defender will do on the ice. Or should do, anyway. When Malkin botches the Triangle Move, it usually is because the defender has made the wrong play, or at least the unanticipated play, rather than the play Malkin already had factored into his personal equation.

Malkin is so hockey smart, he is almost gaming the game. In Crosby's continued absence, Malkin has, after so many seasons, reintroduced himself, stepping into the role of the most dominant, dynamic player in the world . . . and, like the Russian proverb, it is a secret the whole world is beginning to know.

Camouflaged by Crosby's doggedness and technical excellence and dwarfed by the Capitals' Alex Ovechkin's outsized personality and fluency in English, Malkin sometimes hides in plain sight—even though his NHL-best three five-point games this season should make his gifts as apparent as his tape jobs. Malkin, remember, won the Calder Trophy in 2007. He won the scoring title two years later. More significant, he won the Conn Smythe on the '09 Stanley Cup champions.

The brilliance is hardly a scoop. He has been a sublime player practically since he poked a loose puck through Martin Brodeur's pads in October 2006 for his first NHL goal. But as a Wi-Fi outage indirectly reminds us of the wonders of a wired world, we still need an occasional Malkin rampage to notice a player whose brilliance is all too often taken for granted.

Russian Proverb Number 2: *Dva medvedya v odnoi berloge ne zhivut. (Two bears don't lie in one lair.)*

When Malkin arrived in 2006, Crosby, then in his second NHL season, asked the newcomer where he wanted to be in the meticulously choreographed ballet of the Penguins' pregame introductions.

Last. Malkin preferred to be last.

Crosby mentioned he was the final guy but . . . Malkin interrupted. "Three years Super League," he said, and Crosby nodded, ceding pride of place in the time-honored manner to the veteran—even if Malkin had been seasoned 11 time zones away.

Malkin and Crosby are the proverbial bears. They agreeably share a dressing-room lair, perhaps because they read the game at the same expert level. When Crosby is healthy, they work together on the power play. When Pittsburgh presses for a late goal, Malkin often shifts to Crosby's wing. Combining the two best centers on a team since Joe Sakic and Peter Forsberg in Colorado—or maybe Wayne Gretzky and Mark Messier in Edmonton—should make Malkin even more of a threat. Theoretically. "Two of the top five players in the world playing together should be dynamic," Bylsma says. "And the power play should create opportunities for two great players. Why

C, 2006–PRESENT

The second Penguin after Mario Lemieux to be named rookie of the year, he has lived up to the legacy, winning an NHL MVP award, two scoring titles and the playoff MVP in 2009.

hasn't it? I don't have an answer to that. I'm not quite that good of a coach yet."

The curious phenomenon was first noticeable in 2007–08 when Malkin scored 46 points in the 29 games that Crosby missed with an ankle injury. In the 315 games Malkin has played with Crosby in the lineup, he has averaged .435 goals and 1.16 points. In 92 career games without Crosby, Malkin's output jumps significantly—to .630 goals per game and 1.41 points per game. In his first 82 games without Crosby—the length of an NHL regular season, in other words—Malkin had 112 points. In the past decade only five players, including Malkin with an NHL-leading 113 points in '08–09, have surpassed that total.

Malkin possesses what teammate Pascal Dupuis calls the Superman gene. Glasses come off. One-timer comes out. When asked if he would like to appropriate anything from Malkin's

SIZE MATTERS
At 6' 3" and 195 pounds, Malkin has a physique that comes in handy when it is time to protect the puck.

game, Crosby gushes, "There's a lot I would take, starting with his one-timer. . . . I really appreciate his game and really enjoy playing with him." The 5' 11" Crosby would also like some of Malkin's looming size to allow him to protect the puck even better, but he notes, "That's science."

Russian Proverb Number 3: *Kto ne hochet rabotat' letom, budet golodat' zimoi. (They must hunger in winter that will not work in summer.)*

If a hungry Malkin is skating figure eights around the NHL this winter, it is because he did work in summer.

He worked harder than he ever had because for the first time in his 25 years he felt he had no choice. "Maybe before," he says, "little bit lazy," although it was less a case of indolence than the ridiculous ease with which he had mastered hockey. He always had just, you know, played. Then on Feb. 4, 2011, when Sabres defenseman Tyler Myers fell on his right knee in the corner, playtime was over. Malkin had shredded his ACL and MCL. He had surgery. Malkin rehabbed feverishly and even implored Bylsma (to no avail) to play him in Game 7 of the first-round playoff series against the Lightning, a welcome-to-summer 1–0 Pittsburgh loss.

Malkin returned to Russia embarrassed. For the first time in the NHL—indeed for the first time since he was a skinny 19-year-old playing for his hometown team—he had failed to average at least a point per game last season in his 43 matches. More than a streak had vanished. He had

lost his command of the game.

To retrieve something he had once done as well as anyone in the world, he turned to Mike Kadar, the Penguins' strength and conditioning coach. Kadar spent almost three weeks training him in Moscow. Gonchar, who owns a condominium on the same floor there, noticed the zeal with which Malkin embraced the work. "He hadn't always used his talents or pushed 100%," Gonchar says. "The injury helped him mature. It reminded him how much he loved playing the game and made him realize what he had to do to keep playing it at his level. People were forgetting about him [in the discussion of great players]. And that was extra motivation."

Now Malkin's kick-and-giggle games of hallway soccer have been augmented by an actual pregame regimen of stretching. Then he hops over the boards for 21 or so minutes per game and stretches credulity, like he did in mid-February. Fresh off a five-point game a night earlier against the Jets, Malkin scored twice and was on for the other two Pittsburgh goals as he tilted the ice against Tampa Bay in what Bylsma called "our best [example] of playing Pittsburgh Penguins ice hockey." The display of virtuosity was reminiscent not of the other bear in the lair but of co-owner Mario Lemieux.

In Pittsburgh newspapers the next morning Bylsma, Kunitz and defenseman Matt Niskanen were drooling high praise of their fabulous center. Malkin was not made available to the press.

Russian Proverb Number 4: *Horoshaya rabota sama govorit za sebya. (Good work speaks for itself.)* □

GREATEST PENGUINS

FRED VUICH

KRIS LETANG

D, 2006-PRESENT

An offensive force from the blue line, the two-time All-Star has had three seasons of more than 50 points, including a career-best 67 points in 2015-16.

FRED VUICH

CHRIS KUNITZ

LW, 2008-PRESENT

Physical in front of the net and skilled at setting up his teammates—he had 13 assists in the 2009 playoffs—the left wing was a '12-13 All-Star.

C, 2005–PRESENT
After arriving in Pittsburgh to historic hype, Crosby has won two Stanley Cups and nine NHL awards, including the 2013–14 MVP.

SIDNEY CROSBY

Even when he was just 16 years old and playing in Quebec juniors,
it was clear that he was going to be the next big thing

BY MICHAEL FARBER

From Sports Illustrated
October 10, 2003

THIS PRODIGY business isn't fair. Mozart got to play the courts of 18th-century Vienna and Paris and Munich while Sidney Crosby gets the cold arenas of 21st-century Drummondville, Que., and Bathurst, New Brunswick, and Lewiston, Maine. And while Mozart probably never had to carry anything heavier than sheet music, Crosby has to lug his equipment bag full of sweat-soaked gear as he travels the junior hockey hinterland. ¶ You might have heard this said about some other player before, but here goes: Crosby is The Next One. However, you've never heard it from such an authority as The Great One. The 16-year-old center with the tousled black hair and half-smile has been tapped on the shoulder by Wayne Gretzky and told, in effect, Tag! You're it! When asked last summer by The Arizona Republic if a player might one day break some of his NHL scoring records, Gretzky said, "Yes, Sidney Crosby. He's the best player I've seen since Mario [Lemieux]." The anointment was stunning, like Jack Nicklaus's declaration that a 20-year-old Tiger Woods would go on to win more Masters than he and Arnold Palmer combined.

"I was honored Wayne said that," says Troy Crosby, Sidney's father. "It's an honor that he even knows who Sidney is."

Although he won't be eligible for the NHL draft until 2005, Crosby has been on the radar in Canada since his formative years in Cole Harbour, Nova Scotia. He was interviewed by a newspaper reporter for the first time at age seven. He was featured on a segment of CBC's *Hockey Day in Canada* when he was 14. Crosby has been playing against older boys since he was six, and on every team at every level he has put up numbers reminiscent of the days when The Great One and Lemieux were playing wild, wide-open hockey as kids.

In 2002–03 he spent his sophomore year at Shattuck-St. Mary's, a prep school in Faribault, Minn., which is to high school hockey what Harvard is to law school. Then, after

scoring 72 goals in 57 games, he left to play in the Quebec Major Junior Hockey League (QMJHL) and was selected first in the midget draft, by the Rimouski Oceanic, in June. The rumors about Crosby's deal spread like crabgrass. As a 16-year-old rookie he is entitled to the standard $35 per week plus room and board, but there's been a vague whisper that Rimouski is clandestinely paying him $150,000 and has given him an attendance clause in his contract. Troy Crosby and Pat Brisson, Sidney's agent at IMG since June, say they have an agreement with the Oceanic that covers the cost of Sidney's college education only if he chooses to go but insist there is no payment and no attendance clause. That is a pity considering that Rimouski, which was an 11-58-3 doormat that played to many half-empty houses last season, has been a big draw in every arena. On Oct. 16, when Crosby played his first junior game in Nova Scotia, there were 10,189 fans at the Metro Centre in Halifax, 4,000 more than usual. The next night a crowd of 4,574 (including about 400 standing-room-only fans) greeted him in Sydney, Nova Scotia.

"I realize a lot of guys have been tagged with that 'next great player' thing," says Crosby, who is 5' 10" and 185 pounds. "Some have gone on to be great players, some have fallen. I don't want to be one of the guys who disappears."

The burden of being The Next One was a great weight on the last junior player to stir up such a fuss, Eric Lindros. Crosby has been handling it well to this point. He greets the daily interviews with a mix of engagement and caution, always maintaining eye contact and cordially giving answers but not saying much. Crosby knows the drill. He always talks about team goals and shared success. He even dresses in a shirt and tie when he goes to the rink because he remembers New York Rangers general manager Glen Sather saying that if you dress well, you play well.

If Gretzky got his start on his father Walter's backyard rink, Crosby had Troy's 22-by-15-foot basement floor. Troy painted it white, added a red line and a blue line and a regulation four-by-six-foot net. Sidney, who started skating when he was three, was always first-team all-cellar, too good even for his goalie father, who was a 12th-round draft pick of the Montreal Canadiens in 1984. (He never made it to the NHL.) Troy retired from the home basement games when Sidney was nine, because the boy's slappers were leaving him bruised. "He was killing me," says Troy. "I told him, 'You don't need a goalie, just shoot at the net.'"

Troy, a facilities manager for a law firm, put up extra netting behind the goal to protect the basement appliances, but Sidney's shots that missed to the left kept dinging the dryer, which miraculously still works even though it's streaked with puck marks and all the knobs were knocked off.

Dryers aside, no one in the NHL considers the talk about Crosby hot air. He is shifty, fearless and shockingly strong on his skates, but his top attribute might be a remarkable hockey IQ. Crosby's best play in his Halifax homecoming came not while creating both goals in a 2–1 Rimouski win but by backchecking ferociously to strip a streaking Petr Vrana of the puck in the third period. Crosby, a lefthanded shot, used a maneuver called the can opener on the New Jersey Devils' 2003 second-round draft choice. He stuck his stick under Vrana's right armpit, then whacked him on the inside of his left elbow, freeing the puck. That would be a big-time NHL play because, other than Peter Forsberg of the Colorado Avalanche, few big-time NHL players do it with such ease.

Less than 48 hours later Crosby opened some more eyes with a five-point game against Acadie-Bathurst. On one play he swerved to the middle in the offensive zone and then 1) faked a pass that induced the defenseman to drop to the ice; 2) slid the puck under the defenseman as that player went down; 3) hurdled the blueliner without breaking stride; 4) regained control of the puck in the slot; and 5) wheeled to his right while snapping a wrist shot for his second goal. The stunned Bathurst crowd of 3,524 went silent. Suddenly, there was the sound of two hands clapping. A few others joined in, and then more. This was no frenzy—just light rhythmic applause from fans who had been struck by the realization that they had witnessed perhaps the most remarkable goal they are likely to see in their lifetime.

Mark Tobin, a 17-year-old Oceanic left wing, began calling him Gretz, but Crosby quickly put a halt to that. Like Gretzky, he does wear an unusual jersey number—87, because his birth date is 8-7-87—but Crosby says with charming conviction, "I am not Gretz." For the moment, however, he does answer to the nickname Darryl. Tobin came up with that moniker during Rimouski's second preseason game, when Crosby had four goals and four assists. The dazzling offensive show did not eclipse Darryl Sittler's NHL-record 10 points in a game, but, as Tobin says, "It was close enough for me.

"He's a rookie, and we give him crap because of that. But we all know how special he is. We don't come right out and say it, but in our hearts we know one day we'll be telling our grandkids that we played with Sidney Crosby." □

POSTER BOY
Crosby, here taking on the Maple Leafs in 2013, has handled being not just a star but a face of the league.

Sports Illustrated

Editorial Director Christian Stone
Creative Director Christopher Hercik
Director of Photography
Marguerite Schropp Lucarelli

THE PENGUINS AT 50

Editor Bill Syken
Designer Anke Stohlmann
Photo Editor John Blackmar
Writers Michael Farber, Jay Greenberg,
Bob Kravitz, Mark Mulvoy, Jon Scher
Copy Editor Katherine Pradt
Writer-Reporter Jeremy Fuchs
Editorial Production David Sloan, Richard Shaffer

TIME INC. BOOKS
Publisher Margot Schupf
Associate Publisher Allison Devlin
Vice President, Finance Terri Lombardi
Vice President, Marketing Jeremy Biloon
Executive Director, Marketing Services
Carol Pittard
Director, Brand Marketing Jean Kennedy
Sales Director Christi Crowley
Assistant General Counsel Andrew Goldberg
Assistant Director, Production
Susan Chodakiewicz
Senior Manager, Category Marketing
Bryan Christian
Brand Manager Katherine Barnet
Associate Prepress Manager
Alex Voznesenskiy
Project Manager Hillary Leary

Editorial Director Kostya Kennedy
Creative Director Gary Stewart
Director of Photography Christina Lieberman
Editorial Operations Director Jamie Roth Major
Senior Editor Alyssa Smith
Assistant Art Director Anne-Michelle Gallero
Copy Chief Rina Bander
Assistant Managing Editor Gina Scauzillo
Assistant Editor Courtney Mifsud
Special thanks: Brad Beatson, Melissa
Frankenberry, Kristina Jutzi, Simon Keeble,
Seniqua Koger, Kate Roncinske, Kristen Wicker

TERRIBLY GOOD
Game 1 of the 2016
Stanley Cup finals,
just before face-off.

Made in the USA
Columbia, SC
16 October 2017